Nature Guide to
WALLS

JUNE E. CHATFIELD

Contents

Cover photographs:
Top: Red Kite, Welsh Poppy, Puffin
Centre: Spring Squill, Polecat,
Small Pearl-bordered Fritillary
Bottom: Mountains in North Wales viewed
from Hermon in Coed-y-Brenin Forest,
Gwynedd

Edited by Barbara Cork
and Casey Horton

Series Editor: Karen Goaman

Designed by Anne Sharples

The editor wishes to thank Anna Makowiecka and
Pauline Khng, for help in the editorial production
of this book, and Mary Fane for picture research.
The author would also like to thank the following
for their help: Mary Gillham, Steve Moon, Carol
Moxham, Joan Morgan, Wilf Nelson, Charles G
Trew, Adrian Wood, Geoffrey Spencer.

The author and publisher wish to thank the
fóllowing organizations for their help and
guidance: Cardiff Parks Dept., Central Electricity
Generating Board, Countryside Commission,
County Councils and District Councils of Wales,
County Naturalists' Trusts, Field Studies Council,
Forestry Commission, Geological Museum of
North Wales, National Park Authorities, National
Museum of Wales, National Trust, Nature
Conservancy Council, Nurtons Field Centre,
Royal Society for the Protection of Birds, The
Welsh Office, Wales Tourist Board, Welsh Water
Authority.

Most of the illustrations in the section on pages
33–96, Common Species of the Countryside and
Seashore, have been previously published in the
Usborne Spotter's Guides series.

First published in 1981 by
Usborne Publishing Limited
20 Garrick Street, London WC2

© 1981 by Usborne Publishing Limited

Printed and bound in Great Britain by
Fakenham Press Limited, Fakenham, Norfolk

Introduction

Wales is known for the spectacular scenery of its mountains and the dramatic beauty of a superb coastline. It is rich in wildlife and provides a refuge for a number of rare species which include Red Kite, Polecat and arctic-alpine plants such as Purple Saxifrage. The arctic-alpine plants are mostly found high on the rocky crags of Snowdonia – the highest range of mountains in England and Wales. Wales is essentially a mountainous and hilly country where the land use is dominated by sheep farming and extensive forestry plantations.

One of the most interesting features of Wales for the naturalist is the long and varied coastline which surrounds the country on three sides. There are sheltered sandy beaches and coves, rocky shores, and several large muddy estuaries, which are excellent sites for birdwatching. One of the best areas for birdwatching is the Pembrokeshire coast with its offshore islands of Skomer, Skokholm, Grassholm and Ramsey, where vast sea bird colonies (of Razorbills, Gannets, Puffins and Guillemots) are to be seen.

Rivers in mid-Wales often cut deep gorges like this one at Devil's Bridge near Aberystwyth. Oakwoods clothe the steep rocky terrain around.

How to use this Book

The first section of this book, pages 4-32, illustrated with colour photographs and paintings, describes the most interesting wildlife areas of Wales, their characteristic habitats and the animals and plants special to Wales. There are colour maps on pages 4-7 showing the main areas in which the habitats occur. Many habitats are closely linked to the geology and climatic conditions of the country, and these features are also described, on pages 8-9.

The middle section of the book, pages 33-96, contains illustrations of over 350 species of animals and plants commonly found in Wales and over much of Britain. Further details on how to use this section are found on page 33.

The third section of the book, "Places to Visit", found on pages 97-120, consists of a gazetteer containing descriptions of over 150 places of interest. Each county of Wales has a separate list and a map showing the location of the sites. The places described include specific habitats, nature reserves, nature trails, birdwatching points, and also zoos, country parks, gardens, museums and study centres. Further details on how to use this section are found on page 97.

Information such as useful addresses, good reference books, hill safety and a full index are found at the end of the book. Use the index to find out whether a species is illustrated – page numbers referring to illustrations appear in bold.

When visiting the countryside, care should be taken to respect the habitats and the wildlife living there. Flowers should not be picked, nesting birds and mammals with young should not be disturbed, and the Country Code, set out on page 122, should always be followed. Some of the problems related to nature conservation in Wales are also discussed on page 122.

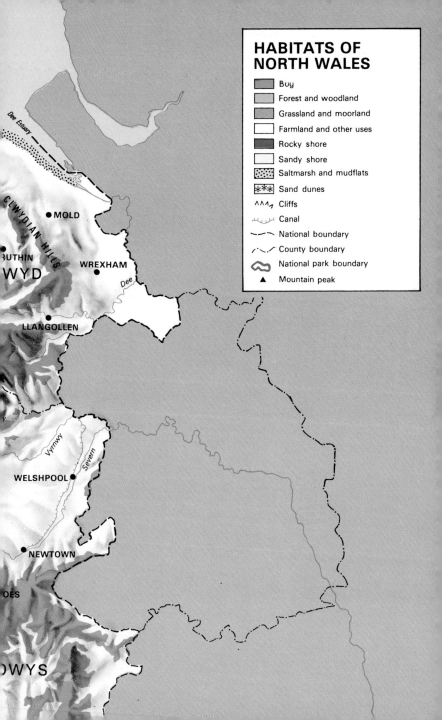

HABITATS OF NORTH WALES

- Bog
- Forest and woodland
- Grassland and moorland
- Farmland and other uses
- Rocky shore
- Sandy shore
- Saltmarsh and mudflats
- Sand dunes
- ^^^ Cliffs
- Canal
- National boundary
- County boundary
- National park boundary
- ▲ Mountain peak

Dee Estuary

CLWYDIAN HILLS

● MOLD

RUTHIN

WYD

● WREXHAM

Dee

● LLANGOLLEN

Vyrnwy

Severn

● WELSHPOOL

● NEWTOWN

OES

OWYS

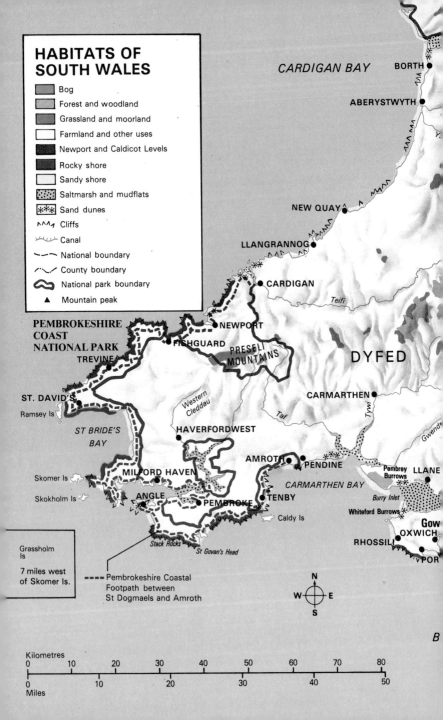

HABITATS OF SOUTH WALES

- Bog
- Forest and woodland
- Grassland and moorland
- Farmland and other uses
- Newport and Caldicot Levels
- Rocky shore
- Sandy shore
- Saltmarsh and mudflats
- Sand dunes
- Cliffs
- Canal
- National boundary
- County boundary
- National park boundary
- ▲ Mountain peak

CARDIGAN BAY

BORTH

ABERYSTWYTH

NEW QUAY

LLANGRANNOG

CARDIGAN

Teifi

PEMBROKESHIRE COAST NATIONAL PARK

NEWPORT

FISHGUARD

PRESELI MOUNTAINS

DYFED

TREVINE

ST. DAVID'S

Ramsey Is

Western Cleddau

St BRIDE'S BAY

HAVERFORDWEST

CARMARTHEN

Taf

Tywi

Gwend

Skomer Is

MILFORD HAVEN

AMROTH

PENDINE

Pembrey Burrows

LLANE

Skokholm Is

ANGLE

PEMBROKE

TENBY

CARMARTHEN BAY

Burry Inlet

Gow

Whiteford Burrows

OXWICH

Caldy Is

RHOSSILI

POR

Stack Rocks

St Govan's Head

Grassholm Is

7 miles west of Skomer Is.

- - - Pembrokeshire Coastal Footpath between St Dogmaels and Amroth

N
W E
S

B

Kilometres
0   10   20   30   40   50   60   70   80

0   10   20   30   40   50
Miles

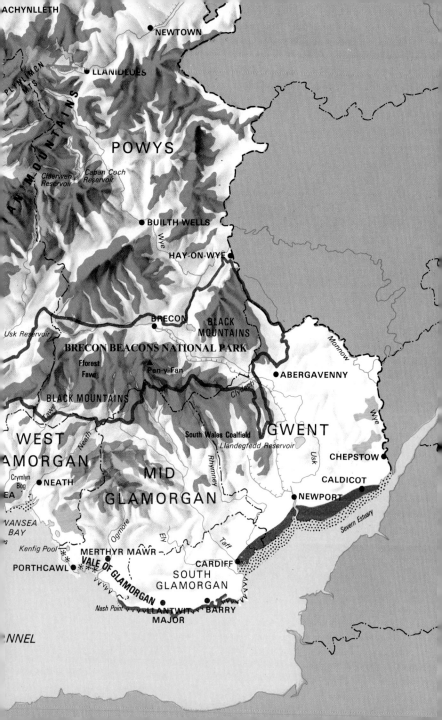

Geology and Climate

Geological Features

Much of the varied scenery of Wales is due to the presence of a wide range of contrasting rocks. In areas such as central Wales the geology tends to be rather uniform, while in other parts, particularly Pembroke, many different rocks occur within a small area, giving diversity to the landscape. The occurrence of different rocks in different areas, together with the climate, influences the distribution of plants and animals.

As much as one third of Wales is made up of slates and shales. Large areas of shale occur in Dyfed, Powys, Gwynedd, and Clwyd and layers of shale may be seen in the cliffs of Cardigan Bay. These rocks are amongst the oldest in Wales and were formed over 400 million years ago.

Shale is a sedimentary rock composed of fine particles laid down in thin layers under water. When shale is subjected to intense pressure it is compressed into slate (a metamorphic rock). Slate is mined extensively in North Wales and there are large quarries in the Llanberis Pass and at Blaenau Ffestiniog.

Other sedimentary rocks found in Wales include sandstones and limestones. Sandstones occur most frequently in the south and south-eastern parts of Wales. The colourful red soils often seen in this part of the country are due to the weathering of a rock known as Old Red Sandstone. Old Red Sandstones form the Brecon Beacons and the Black Mountains, and are also exposed in cliffs in the Pembroke area. The high ground of the Welsh coalfield is composed of a different, less colourful sandstone (Coal Measures) and some layers contain seams of coal. This coal-bearing rock is responsible for the industrial history of South Wales. The coal is mined by both shaft and open cast methods.

Limestones are absent from the central regions of Wales and are of limited distribution elsewhere. These rocks are often rich in fossils, and the different types of limestone are identified by the fossils they

▼ Rugged limestone cliffs near St Govan's Head, Pembroke coast. The sea has exploited joints and other weaknesses in the rock to form caves, and isolated pillars of rock (sea stacks).

contain. Carboniferous Limestone is a hard block-like rock which produces a rugged landscape and is often associated with spectacular scenery. In Wales it occurs mainly in coastal areas in the south, the north-east and Anglesey. It contains fossils of corals and other sea creatures called crinoids. Different limestones are found in the Welsh Borderland and form a plateau in the Vale of Glamorgan.

The Glamorgan coast near Barry has the best exposures of the sedimentary rocks known as breccia (consolidated rock fragments) and colourful fine-grained rocks known as marls.

In Anglesey, Snowdonia, the Preseli Mountains and on the Lleyn Peninsula, igneous rocks form striking scenery. These rocks were formed beneath the earth's surface from molten rock, which sometimes pushed into cracks in other rock beds. Igneous rocks may be changed by heat and pressure into metamorphic rocks and these are represented in Wales by hornblende schists on Anglesey.

Climate

The attractive greenness of much of the Welsh countryside is due to the mild, damp climate that is characteristic of the western Atlantic coast of Europe. The amount of rainfall varies from one area to another and is affected by altitude. The lowland areas have over 1000 mm a year while the upland regions receive twice as much. Snowdonia is the wettest area with about 2600 mm a year; some of this is accounted for by winter snow on the mountain peaks.

The Gulf Stream, which flows from the warm waters of the Gulf of Mexico, passes up the western side of the British Isles. It has a warm influence along the coast of Wales, particularly in the south-west. The temperature and changes in season are also affected by altitude. It is possible, for example, to drive from the Vale of Glamorgan when the leaves are nearly out on the hedgerows, and arrive the same day in Snowdonia to a scene reminiscent of winter with the trees completely bare.

▼ Striking cliffs at Llantwit Major in south Glamorgan. Horizontal layers of Liassic Limestone are dissected by vertical joints causing blocks of rock to break away from the cliff. The hard limestone layers are separated by thinner layers of loose shale. The Devil's Toe Nail, a type of fossil Oyster, is found at Nash Point.

▲ Ceibwr Bay, near Cardigan, showing rock folds in the cliffs. The grits and shales were contorted into this shape millions of years ago.

▼ Coal Measure Sandstones at Saundersfoot, near Tenby. The layers of rock have been pushed up into a steep fold or anticline and the sea has eaten away at the weakest point to make a cave.

Snowdonia

Some of the most spectacular scenery in Wales is found in the Snowdonia National Park. Deep river valleys cut through the mountains, providing passes for roads and adding to the dramatic appearance of the area. The landscape is also enhanced by numerous mountain lakes, and hanging and U-shaped valleys formed by glaciers during the series of Ice Ages of the last million years. Much of the land is over 600 metres (2000 feet), while the summit of Snowdon reaches 1085 metres (3560 feet).

Moorland, Grassland and Mountain Peaks

The mountain moorlands are characterized by coarse tufts of Mat Grass; only a limited range of wild plants can grow here owing to the acid rocks that form much of Snowdonia. It is on the relatively mineral-rich igneous rocks that the more interesting wild flowers are found and these, particularly the special arctic-alpine plants, have attracted botanists to the area since the eighteenth century. Cwm Idwal is a particularly famous site for arctic-alpine flowers.

A few rare mountain flowers are able to survive on cold, windswept crags; most of them are small and grow close to the ground or in crevices. Typical arctic-alpine and mountain flowers of Snowdonia include Roseroot, Snowdon Lily, Globeflower, Alpine Meadow-rue, Mountain Sorrel, Hairy Rockcress, several species of saxifrage, Dwarf Willow and Golden-rod. Of the various saxifrages, the Tufted Saxifrage is a rare species. The yellow Welsh Poppy grows on rock ledges in the mountains with these arctic-alpine plants, but is also found on lower ground. In all, about 900 species of flowers, trees and grasses have been noted in the Park.

The mountain grasslands, like the moorlands, have a limited vegetation due to the predominantly acid soil. Where spring waters have come into contact with less acid rocks, extra minerals are brought to the surface. These fertile "flush areas" often support a wider range of plants,

▼ View of Moel Siabod from Cnicht, which is east of the main Snowdon range. Siabod is made of slate with a hard igneous cap; a few arctic-alpine plants grow on calcareous rock outcrops.

especially lush growths of mosses.

The highest mountain summits have little soil and only a few plants can survive there. Where the terrain consists of rock and screes, lichens establish on the surface of the rocks, while Woolly Hair Moss, *Racomitrium*, forms extensive carpets on rock rubble. This moss is typical of mountain regions; equally characteristic is the Map Lichen, which forms yellow-green patches on boulders.

Some of the rocks in Snowdonia contain heavy metals such as lead and gold that have been exploited commercially, while peat deposits at Hermon in the Coed-y-Brenin Forest contain a high copper content. Trees cannot thrive in these copper-rich areas but a rather unusual assemblage of plants has become established.

At Hermon, Thrift and Spring Sandwort, two flowers that are normally limited to the seashore, grow with dense hummocks of tufted *Cladonia* lichens.

The birds of Snowdonia include some species that are not generally distributed in lowland areas: the Raven and Chough may be seen on high ground and the Red Grouse where there is heather moorland. The Ring Ouzel is a typical mountain bird and is much the same size as the Blackbird. Predatory Peregrine Falcons and Merlins, which were once numerous, are now rarely seen. Common small birds include Wheatear and Meadow Pipits. The Curlew, a large wading bird of salt-marshes, is also seen in the hills where it breeds in summer. The presence of the Curlew is often detected by its loud call.

▼ These arctic-alpine plants grow in the mountains of Snowdonia on rock ledges and scree slopes where there is little competition from other plants and they are out of reach of grazing animals. They flower during June and July. The Parsley Fern is rare in Wales outside Snowdonia; the fronds turn rusty brown in autumn.

Parsley Fern

Snowdon Lily

Globeflower

Map Lichen

Purple Saxifrage

Roseroot

Woodland and Lake

Much of Snowdonia was once forested but now most of it is rough mountain pasture. The existing wooded areas consist mainly of plantations of coniferous trees managed by the Forestry Commission. As these are planted with introduced as well as native trees they are ideal places to see and identify many different trees. A few remnants of the native Sessile Oak woods survive in some places and these woods can be explored along the nature trails in the Gwydir Forest near Llanrwst and at Maentwrog. (Sessile Oak differs from English Oak in the stalkless acorns and the longer stalk on the leaf.)

Oakwoods in Snowdonia are fairly open with a vegetation of grass, Bilberry and luxuriant growths of mosses on woodland banks and tree trunks. Ferns are plentiful, with Male Fern, Lady Fern, Hard Fern, Hart's-tongue, Common Polypody and Broad Buckler on trees and ground, but the growth of wild flowers in many of these Oakwoods is sometimes restricted by sheep grazing.

A wide variety of birds live in Oakwoods, amongst them several species of tits including Blue Tits, Coal Tits, Long-tailed Tits and Willow Tits. Pied Flycatchers, Redstarts, Nuthatches, Treecreepers, Wrens, Chaffinches and Great Spotted and Green Woodpeckers may also be seen amongst the leaves and branches. Unlike the Oakwoods, mature conifer plantations are dark and therefore the wildlife is limited, although Goldcrests and Crossbills nest in these woods. However, in a large forest there are usually open areas where trees have been felled and replanted. Young plantations encourage a wide range of birds – Meadow Pipits, Whinchats, Yellowhammers, Willow Warblers, Chaffinches – and butterflies, particularly Speckled Wood. Voles and Shrews live in the grass under the young trees and these provide food for predators such as Kestrels and Buzzards.

Woodland areas are a stronghold for both the native Red Squirrel and the American Grey Squirrel although unfortunately the number of native squirrels is declining. The Pine Marten was once a common animal in North Wales but is now rare; the visitor is more likely to see the Polecat, which is similar in appearance.

▼ Pied Flycatchers are summer visitors to Welsh uplands; they often nest in holes in trees. The male (*right*) grows striking black and white feathers in the breeding season.

▼ The Gwydir Forest north of Betws-y-Coed includes some native Oakwoods on rocky terrain. The wet climate of this part of Wales favours the growth of ferns, mosses and liverworts.

▲ The Raven walks and hops rather clumsily on the ground but is an accomplished acrobat in the air, particularly during the breeding season.

▲ The Ring Ouzel or Mountain Blackbird is a summer visitor to Wales and breeds in the uplands. The nest is hidden in heather or rocks.

▲ The tiny Goldcrest is a restless and agile bird that frequents woods and plantations. It is difficult to spot as it feeds in the tops of trees.

▲ The Mistle Thrush often builds its nest of moss, grasses and roots in the fork of a tree. The young are fed on insect larvae and worms.

▲ Kestrels nest from April to July; they may rear their young in an abandoned Crow's nest.

▲ Male Crossbill: the hooked beak is used to open fir or pine cones to reach the seeds inside.

▼ The Speckled Wood emerges in April-May; it occurs in shady woodland edges and rides.

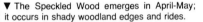

▼ Welsh Poppies often grow with arctic-alpine plants on rocky mountain ledges in Snowdonia.

Polecats are quite numerous in Wales and dead ones are occasionally found at road-sides. More common are the Foxes, Hares and Rabbits, which also live in mountain habitats .

In recent years the Forestry Commission has opened up many of its forests as amenity areas, providing picnic and parking sites, nature trails and visitors' centres. It is important to appreciate that forestry is a commercial activity and great care should be taken to prevent fires. Once started, forest fires may burn for several days and involve a heavy financial loss in addition to the immeasurable damage that they cause to wildlife.

Lakes in North Wales range from small mountain tarns to large lakes which often serve as reservoirs. Bala Lake, the largest natural lake in Wales, is known for the Gwyniad (freshwater Whiting), and the Llanberis Lakes are known for the rare Char. Minnows are the common fish of upland lakes and Brown Trout are found everywhere in streams.

Although the mountains have the appearance of a natural wild habitat, the ecology of the Snowdonia area has been influenced by man for centuries. In addition to the decline of the old Oakwoods, the number and range of many of the mountain plants have decreased due partly to over-collecting, and also to over-grazing by sheep and goats from the hill farms.

▲ Wales is the last remaining stronghold for the Polecat, a nocturnal hunter that preys on small mammals, birds and frogs. It was once wide-spread in Britain but is now almost extinct in England although it is quite common in Wales.

▲ The Brown Hare lives on open farmland and moorland in Wales. It is normally a solitary and silent animal and usually spends the day above ground in a hollow or "form", coming out to feed on grass, grain or roots at dusk.

▼ The Pine Marten is one of Britain's rarest mammals. It is a shy animal that hunts at night emerging at dusk to prey on small mammals, birds and insects. It is an agile climber and lives in mountain woods in north-west Wales.

▼ The Red Squirrel lives mostly in coniferous woods in Wales but its numbers have decreased this century due to the destruction of its habitat. The Red Squirel is active in the day but is difficult to spot since it is a shy animal.

Brecon Beacons

Brecon Beacons National Park is well known for the wild and largely unspoilt beauty of its countryside. The Park is mainly mountainous with the dominant peaks formed by Fforest Fawr, the Brecon Beacons and Black Mountains. The River Usk, flowing through the Brecons, has created a wide flat valley, while elsewhere the River Neath and its tributaries have been responsible for some spectacular waterfalls and limestone caves. Although many people visit the Park for its scenery, the lakes, woods, hills, moors and wetlands are rich in wildlife and provide excellent sites for the naturalist.

The Uplands

Much of the land in the Brecon Beacons consists of acid moorland and grassland that is grazed by sheep. Most of the hills are dominated by grasses and, in a few places, by Bell Heather and Ling. Bilberry, Gorse and Bracken add their particular colours to the landscape at various seasons. The abundance and diversity of the upland plant species are very much affected by the degree of sheep grazing.

Over 200 species of birds have been recorded in the National Park and about half of this number have bred here. Their presence varies according to the season and the weather conditions. Summer is the best time to watch for the birds of the high hills. Several birds of prey may be seen hovering or skimming over the grassy upland slopes, especially Kestrels and Buzzards with the occasional Merlin and Peregrine Falcon and, rarely, the Red Kite. Other upland birds to look out for are Wheatears, Ring Ouzels, Curlews, Snipe, Red Grouse, and Ravens.

Mountain tops in the Brecon Beacons can be very windswept and inhospitable. It is here that the arctic-alpine plants grow, often on bare rock ledges where they are out of the reach of sheep. In the Brecons, arctic-alpine plants are at the southern extent of their range in the British Isles; fewer arctic-alpine species are found here than in Snowdonia. The wild mountain

▼ The summit of Bannau Sir Gaer with screes below the steep walls of Old Red Sandstone rock. The flat summit is also found on surrounding peaks; it is due to a hard layer of quartz conglomerate.

flowers of the Brecons include the Purple Saxifrage, Dwarf Willow, Roseroot, Mossy Saxifrage, Globeflower and the Lesser Meadow-rue. Green Spleenwort and Parsley Fern are two of the mountain ferns.

Lakes, Streams and Canals

An abundance of plant and animal species is found in and around the still waters of Llangorse Lake (*Llyn Safaddan*) which lies south-east of Brecon. The extensive vegetation and varied animal life are due to an ample supply of minerals in the alkaline water. Birds are attracted to the reed beds and waterside shrubs, for these provide them with protected areas for roosting and nesting. Great Crested Grebes, Little Grebes and Herons feed on the fish of the lake, Warblers and Reed Buntings may be seen in the marginal reeds and Yellow Wagtails at the water's edge. Birds likely to be found here in the winter are Goosander, Whooper and Bewick's Swans, Pintail, Canada Goose and various waders. Llangorse Lake is also one of the few sites in Wales where the rare Fringed Water-lily may be seen. Water Snails thrive in the lime-rich waters of the Lake; their shells are found washed up on the shores.

Mountain tarns and reservoirs also form large bodies of still water in the Brecon Beacons. Tal-y-bont, near Brecon itself, is perhaps the most interesting of the reservoirs as it is a good site for birdwatching, particularly for waders and wildfowl. Many of these waters, however, support a limited variety of aquatic life as they are acid and deficient in minerals. Consequently there is little food for birds that feed in the water.

▲ Red Grouse live on heather moorland where they feed on young heather shoots. They are well camouflaged by their mottled plumage.

▲The Fringed Water-lily grows in deep water and its floating stems may reach 1.5 metres (five feet). It flowers in mid-summer.

▼ Purple Loosestrife grows in marshes and beside rivers and lakes in south and west Wales. Its tall flowering spikes appear in mid-summer.

▼ Merlins are rare birds in most of Britain but nest on Welsh moors in summer. They may be seen in flight pursuing small birds or perching on rocks or fence posts.

▲ The Grey Heron nests in large colonies near water in most parts of Wales. The bulky and untidy nest is built high in trees; the male usually brings twigs to the female and she builds the nest. Each pair rears three to five young.

▲ Snipe live on marshland and other wetland areas where they probe deep in the mud for worms and insect larvae. Large numbers arrive from north-west Europe in the winter to swell the size of the resident Welsh population.

▼ Llangorse Lake (Llyn Safaddan) is a large natural lake formed during the last Ice Age. The Black Mountains dominate the skyline to the east, while the immediate surroundings of the lake consist of a patchwork of fertile fields that take advantage of the richer soil of the lake basin. Llangorse Lake is now a popular recreational area for all kinds of water sports but is also a site of great interest to the naturalist for birds and lakeside plants. The lake is fed by the River Llynfi.

Many springs emerge from the hills and flow down as rushing, stony streams. A characteristic bird of both streams and rivers is the small Dipper, which habitually perches on boulders in mid-stream. In the streams there are freshwater Shrimps, Blackfly and Caddisfly larvae, and Limpets attached to stones. A very similar range of animals lives in the fast-flowing, boulder-strewn rivers such as the Usk, as the environmental conditions are much the same as those of the streams.

Wales has very few canals but the attractive Brecon and Abergavenny Canal follows the Usk valley through the Park, passing the Brecon Beacons and Black Mountains. It was once allowed to become derelict but has been renovated and is now a popular waterway for pleasure boats. The canal contains a variety of water plants and numerous Dragonfly nymphs. These nymphs, once they mature, change into graceful insects, seen on the wing, over the water and marginal vegetation in summer. More slender are the Damselflies, common in the Brecon Beacons and easily noticed by their iridescent blue bodies. Iridescent-blue is also seen in the plumage of the Kingfisher, which frequents the canal and the River Usk.

Woodlands

Deciduous woodland once covered the Brecon Beacons but most of these native forests were cleared long ago to make way for arable and grazing land. However some small remnants of natural woodland are hidden away in deep gorges around the edge of the Park. These remaining woodlands give some indication of the

▲ The Dipper is a typical bird of mountain streams. It dives and swims to feed.

▲ The Small Pearl-bordered Fritillary flies in June and July. It favours open areas in woods.

▼ Common Blue Damselflies prey on small insects near lakes, ponds and canals in summer.

▼ Common Toads hibernate over the winter; in spring they migrate to ponds and ditches to breed.

▼ At dusk, Badgers follow well-worn paths from their underground setts to search for food.

geology and type of soil present in the area. Oak, particularly western Sessile Oak, dominates the deciduous woodlands on the acid soils of Old Red Sandstone while Ashwoods occur on more alkaline soils.

The distinctive orange-berried Rowan or Mountain Ash is a common tree in the Welsh hills but its relatives, the White-beams, include three species that are not found anywhere outside the National Park. They thrive on the limestone in the Cwm Clydach Reserve near Abergavenny. The Reserve also has one of the few native Beechwoods in Wales; most of the other Beechwoods in Wales have been planted.

Spring is the best time to explore the woodlands for wild flowers. The number of different plants that grow on the woodland floor is determined partly by the nature of the soil and partly by the density of the overhanging tree canopy. Most woodland herbs leaf and flower early in the year, before the trees come into full leaf and block out the source of light. Many of the plants are visited by a number of wood-land butterflies – Green-veined White, Small Pearl-bordered Fritillary, and the Meadow Brown. Woodland butterflies frequent open glades and clearings, the edges of woods and wide forest rides.

Bogs

In the Brecon Beacons, boggy, peaty areas are found on the upland moors and in the valley bottoms. Bogs develop on acid and water-logged soils and support some interesting plant species peculiar to this environment. Mosses are usually the dominant plants and cover much of the area. The most characteristic bog plant is Sphagnum Moss, some 30 species of which are found in Britain. These species of mosses not only differ in appearance but also grow in different moisture zones of the bog in which they live. Some grow on hummocks, some grow at the edge of the bog and others are restricted to pools. Growing with and amongst these mosses are flowering plants and grasses, particularly the Cotton or Bog Grasses – members of the sedge family – and Purple Moor-grass, which may sometimes take over from Sphagnum as the dominant species.

Some bog plants have developed an insectivorous way of life. This is possibly an adaptation to the low level of mineral nutrients in the soil. Insectivorous plants include Sundew and Butterwort, both of which trap insects on their leaves. Other notable and attractive bog plants are Bog Asphodel, Bogbean and Marsh Orchid, all of which flower in summer.

▼ Bog Asphodel has star-like flowers that grow in tall spikes on leafless stems.

▼ The Kingfisher nests in holes in river banks and dives into the water to catch fish.

Pembrokeshire Coast

The Pembrokeshire Coast National Park includes the long-distance footpath along the coast. The path crosses many cliffs, estuaries, saltmarshes, rocky shores, and sand dunes and gives magnificent views of caves, sea stacks and other unusual rock features. It also provides access to stretches of the coast that cannot be reached by road. Off the shore there are several small islands where vast numbers of sea birds may be seen. With its wealth of wildlife this is undoubtedly one of the best places in Wales to study marine life.

The northern part of the Park extends inland to include the Preseli Mountains and in the south it incorporates the upper reaches of Milford Haven. This southern region has a particularly mild climate with a lower rainfall than most of Wales and several species of Mediterranean plants and animals are able to live here. An example is the southern European Sandhill Snail, which is common at Tenby.

The Coastal Footpath

Sea birds are a feature all the way along the coastal footpath, particularly those that nest on cliffs. Fulmars nest at Trevine and are found in over a dozen other sites; Choughs are less common but they can occur along any part of the path. On cliffs and sea stacks Razorbills, Guillemots, Kittiwakes and Shags may be seen and these also live in large colonies at Stack Rocks near Castlemartin. In the autumn wading birds migrate to Pembrokeshire from the north.

In spring and summer the cliffs are bright with wild flowers and butterflies. Typical plants include Thrift, Buckshorn, Plantain, Golden Samphire and Rock Samphire, Rock Sea-lavender, English Stonecrop, Sea Campion, Spring Squill, and Scurvy-grass, as well as other common, attractive flowers of the wayside. Day-flying Burnet and Cinnabar Moths feed on the cliff-top flowers.

▼ Whitesand Bay near St David's. The rocks on the foreshore are colonized by brown seaweeds, such as Serrated Wrack, and the red seaweed, Dulse. Barnacles also cement themselves to the rocks.

▲ Puffins may be seen on grassy, coastal cliffs or offshore islands from April to early August. They make their nests in burrows in the ground.

▲ The huge Great Black-backed Gull is a fierce hunter, killing Puffins and Shearwaters as well as Rabbits. It breeds on rocky coasts in Wales.

▲ Gannets breed in colonies on rocky islands; adults are distinguished by a yellowish head.

▲ Guillemots rear their young on cliff ledges; adults fence in the chicks for protection.

▼ Razorbills nest on cliffs and rocky shores in west Wales. They are expert divers and underwater swimmers. In summer they gather in large groups on the sea for an elaborate courtship display.

Butterflies include the Brimstone, Common Blue, Pearl-bordered Fritillary, Dark Green Fritillary, Large Skipper, Small Tortoiseshell and Painted Lady. Some of these are migrants from the Continent, augmenting the native population.

Skylarks soar over the cliff tops and other small land birds – Stonechats, Meadow Pipits, Yellowhammers, Dunnocks, Chaffinches, and Bullfinches – are found amongst the shrubs.

The Islands

The offshore islands of Skomer, Skokholm, Grassholm, and Ramsey are a feature of the Pembrokeshire coast and are well-known for the richness of their bird life and cliff-top flowers. Skomer and Ramsey are nature reserves and are served by a regular boat service. Skomer, managed by the West Wales Naturalists' Trust, has large colonies of Fulmars, Shags, Kittiwakes, Razorbills, Puffins, Herring and Greater and Lesser Black-backed Gulls. Pairs of nocturnal Manx Shearwaters, which spend the day hidden in burrows underground, may be seen in flight by those who stay overnight on the island.

Land birds include Short-eared Owls and Buzzards, which feed on the numerous Voles, Mice and Shrews of the grassland and scrub. Skomer is especially noted for the Skomer Vole, its own subspecies of Bank Vole, but these elusive animals are unlikely to be seen. Grey Seals bob up and down in the sea and come to the shore of Skomer and Ramsey Islands to breed in late summer and autumn.

Ramsey Island, reached by boat from St Justinian, has a similar range of sea birds as well as Ravens, Choughs, Oystercatchers, Lapwings, predatory birds such as Owls and Kestrels, and small land birds. Grassholm Island is an RSPB Nature Reserve and has a large breeding colony of Gannets, one of the largest in the British Isles. Skokholm is also a bird reserve. It is managed by the West Wales Naturalists' Trust and access is limited to parties staying on the island. It is noted for its large colonies of Storm Petrel.

Sandy and Rocky Shores

Some parts of the shore (notably at Pendine, Tenby, Freshwater West, Stackpole, and Newport) are backed by sand dunes, which support many interesting plants and animals, while the rocky shores exhibit a wide range of seaweeds and marine animals. European Cowries may be found at low water during spring tides; colourful Sea Slugs may also be found here. Dwarf Winkles and Rough Winkles live in small crevices on the cliffs at high water mark. Further down the shore on rocks and in rock pools, there is greater variety. Four species of Topshell live on the shore and one of these, the Thick Topshell, is restricted to south-west England and the coast of Wales. Low on the shore and in the shelter of caves are Sponges, Sea Squirts, and Sea Mats.

▼ The Linnet (*left*) lives in open bushy country and on the coast. It often nests in Gorse bushes. Short-eared Owls (*centre*) nest regularly on Skomer; the nest is hidden in heather or grass. The Storm Petrel (*right*) feeds at sea during the day but returns to its nesting burrow at night.

▲ The Painted Lady breeds in Britain but migrates to North Africa for the cold winter months. The caterpillars feed on Spear Thistle.

▲ Orange Tips are common in damp meadows and hedgerows from May to July. Only the male has the orange wing patches.

▲ Wheatears are active restless birds that breed in open country in Wales in the summer. They nest on cliffs, screes and in holes in walls.

▲ Manx Shearwaters breed in large colonies on Skomer and Skokholm from March to August. They often form large "rafts" on the sea at dusk.

▲ Bottle-nosed Dolphins may be seen swimming off the Welsh coast, especially in summer.

▲ Grey Seals usually live out at sea but form breeding colonies on rocky coasts in autumn.

▼ Star Sea Squirts live in colonies; the whole colony is enclosed in a jelly-like tunic.

▼ The Thick Topshell has a blunt white "tooth" inside the mouth opening of its shell.

Some of the sandy beaches of Pembrokeshire are very exposed, with surf waves breaking along the shore, and these sands support little marine life. Less exposed are beaches at Newport, St Bride's Bay, Saundersfoot, Tenby, and Pendine; here a wide range of sea shells are washed up and some live in the sands of the shore. Wading birds and gulls feed on the animal life of the sand when it is exposed by the tide, and the waders also feed on the saltmarshes and mudflats that are a particular feature upstream from Milford Haven. Seawater penetrates inland up the estuary for several miles and this is indicated by seaweed attached to the shore near high water. Saltmarshes are curiously attractive places; they are colonized only by plants and animals that can tolerate an occasional submerging in saltwater.

Preseli Mountains

While the coast and islands are a major attraction of Pembrokeshire, the inland country is also of considerable interest. The stone circles and burial chambers, including a fine one at Pentre Ifan, are evidence that these wild, open spaces have been used by man for centuries.

The Preseli Mountains have an acid soil, with large areas of moorland, on which sheep and ponies graze, and with bogs in areas of poor drainage. The moorlands are covered by Bell Heather and Ling as well as Bilberry, Bracken and the small western species of Gorse, *Ulex gallii*. The birds are rather similar to those of the Brecon Beacons, with many small birds such as Skylarks on the moorland, and Buzzards, Kestrels and Ravens overhead. Ring Ouzel and Merlin occasionally frequent the area.

▼ Rock Sea Spurrey grows on cliffs, rocks and walls by the sea on the west coast of Wales.

▲ Fleabane is a plant of marshes, wet meadows, ditches and hedgerows. It flowers from August to September. The smoke from burning Fleabane is supposed to drive away fleas.

▼ The rare Tree Mallow grows on the west coast of Wales on rocks, waste ground or offshore sea stacks, especially those with colonies of gulls or auks. It may reach three metres in height.

Gower

Gower is a peninsula in South Wales situated just west of Swansea. Scenically very attractive, it has a great variety of plants and animals, and these include some national rarities. Along the coast there are prominent headlands, while inland the land is fairly level and much of it forms a limestone plateau. On this small peninsula the sea is never very far away and many of the hedgerows are bent to one side by the prevailing west winds.

Coastal Cliffs and Sand Dunes

Along the south coast, footpaths follow the cliff tops and provide access to the rocks below. The Gower cliffs are of special interest for the spray-tolerant plants such as Golden and Rock Samphire, and Rock Sea-lavender. In spring the cliffs are colourful with flowers such as Spring Squill and Early Purple Orchid. Butterflies take advantage of the warm southern slopes and feed on the nectar of wild flowers. Ravens and Jackdaws soar over the cliffs and Cormorants fish out at sea.

A wide range of wild flowers are found on sand dunes. There are extensive sand dune systems at Oxwich Bay, Whiteford, Broughton and Llangennith Burrows; smaller patches occur at Rhossili, Port Eynon, Horton, and Pennard. Dunes are formed from dry sand carried by the wind.

At the top of the beach, near the sea, low accumulations of sand can be seen, and in this zone of foredunes, a limited range of plants such as the succulent Sea Sandwort, the prickly Saltwort, Sea Rocket, and Sand Couchgrass can establish. Taller mounds of sand near the shore are stabilized by underground stems of Marram Grass. This is the "yellow dune zone" where sand is still being deposited. In addition to Marram Grass there is Sea Spurge, Sea Holly and Rest-harrow.

Further away from the sea is the zone of "grey dunes", which have a complete and stable turf composed of a larger range of plants. Lichens and mosses cover bare ground and Bracken and Dewberry (a non-glossy Blackberry) grow in some areas.

▼ Three Cliffs Bay is a sandy beach just east of Oxwich on the south Gower coast. It is encircled by cliffs of Carboniferous Limestone and there is a small saltmarsh beside the stream.

▲ The liquid trill of the Skylark, singing as it soars high overhead, is one of the sounds of summer on the dunes of the Gower coast.

▲ Male Stonechat in summer breeding plumage; the female is a pale mottled brown. They are found on gorse heaths, moors and on the coast.

▲ Male Eider Duck in breeding plumage; the female is brown, mottled and barred with black. Eider Ducks are regular visitors to the Burry Inlet.

▲ Oystercatchers are common birds of the coast. They use their powerful beaks to prise open Cockles and Mussels and probe for worms.

▲ Shelduck are common on mudflats and marshes. Both sexes have the colourful plumage.

▲ Rock Pipits may be seen at the top of rocky beaches. They nest from late April to June.

▼ The Yellow Whitlow Grass is a rare plant that grows only on the Gower coast.

▼ Pyramidal Orchids grow on sand dunes and grassland; they flower from June to August.

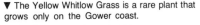

Plants of the dunes typically flower early in the year while the sand is still moist, mainly in May and June.

Dune systems are very vulnerable to destruction since a break in the vegetation cover followed by drying of the sand can lead to large, hollow "blow-outs" down to the level of damp sand. One of the colonizing plants seen in blow-outs is the Sand Sedge, which puts out shoots from its long underground stem in extraordinarily straight lines. In hollows where the sand is permanently moist, (dune slacks) a different range of plants is to be seen. The characteristic colonizer of the slacks is Creeping Willow, but in season there are a variety of orchids – the Southern Marsh Orchid, Marsh Helleborine, Pyramidal Orchid, Green-winged Orchid, Autumn Lady's Tresses and Fen Orchid. Common Centaury, Yellow-wort, Rest-harrow, and Felwort also grow in the slacks.

Various small birds live in dunes, principally Skylarks, Meadow Pipits, and Stonechats, which all nest on the ground. Snail shells are likely to be noticed on sand or attached to plants; yellow or pink shells (often striped) of the Brown-lipped Snail are common on dunes, together with those of the Common Garden Snail.

Saltmarshes

Saltmarshes and mudflats occur along the north coast of Gower near Llanrhidian. There are several zones of marsh development, from bare muddy sand to an intertidal zone of Cord-grass and succulent Glasswort, and near the top of the shore a higher zone of more stable mud with a turf of fine-leaved Sea Poa grass and Sea Rush. Around pools and in the upper marsh grow Glasswort, Annual Seablite, Sea Purslane and Sea Aster.

A limited range of animals live on saltmarshes but those that do are very abundant. The Laver Spire Snail lives in dense colonies on the Llanrhidian Marsh where wading birds feed on it.

▼ Saltmarshes develop in sheltered areas, especially estuaries. The colonizing plants can tolerate high salt concentrations and trap silt and mud which builds up the level of the marsh.

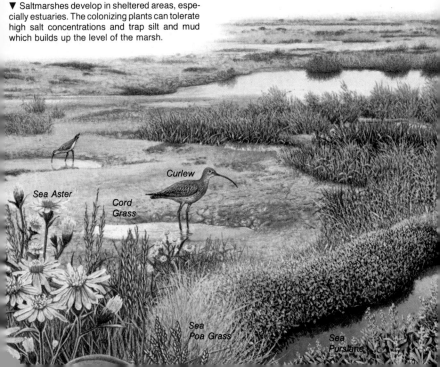

Sea Aster

Curlew

Cord Grass

Sea Poa Grass

Sea Purslane

The mudflats are good places to look for birds, especially in the winter. Wildfowl include Eider Duck and Brent Goose and there are wading birds such as Redshank, Oystercatcher and Curlew; the calls of Curlew and Redshank are a feature of the saltings.

Inland

Moorland vegetation is established inland in some areas. Where the drainage is impeded, plants typical of bogs may be found. Broad Pool on Cillibion has been made a nature reserve, since the rare Fringed Water-lily grows there. Walls, particularly in sheltered lanes, provide suitable places for many flowering plants such as Wall Pennywort, and Ivy-leaved Toadflax, while numerous snails, woodlice and spiders live in the crevices. Stonechats, Yellowhammers and other small birds perch amongst the bushes in open country.

A number of woodlands are established on Gower and many of these are a mixture of Oak and Ash. Plants on the woodland floor include Wood Anemone, Wood Sorrel, Wood Sanicle, Bluebell, Wood Garlic, Lords and Ladies, Dog's Mercury, and in some places, Herb Paris.

Silver-washed Fritillary and Speckled Wood are two butterflies found in woodland glades. Other butterflies on Gower include Gatekeeper, Small Heath, Grayling, Wall Brown, Peacock, Small Copper, Common and Small Blue.

▼ Semi-wild Welsh Ponies live and breed on saltmarshes on the north coast of Gower and also at Three Cliffs Bay. During low tide the ponies move on to the lower marsh to feed.

▲ Bluebells grow in spectacular blue carpets on woodland floors and grassy cliffs in spring.

▲ Wood Anemones flower in deciduous woods in spring, before the trees come into leaf.

▲ Bugle is common in damp woods and grassy places. It often grows in large patches since it spreads easily by means of creeping runners.

▼ Wood Garlic grows in damp shady places in woods and thickets, usually forming a carpet of white flowers. It smells strongly of garlic.

Vale of Glamorgan

To the east of Swansea is the Vale of Glamorgan, a plateau of limestone with a cliffed coastline and coastal footpaths. The limestone is evident in the buildings and in the old walls where a number of interesting plants grow, particularly ferns. Protruding from many damp crevices are ferns such as the Common Polypody, Maidenhair Spleenwort, Hart's-tongue, Rusty-back, and Wall-rue. Wall Pennywort is a distinctive flowering plant which is characteristic of walls in the west of Britain while Ivy-leaved Toadflax, mosses and lichens are also conspicuous colonizers. Some of the walls in this area are of special interest as they have large fossil ammonites set into them.

Two good sand dune areas occur in the Vale of Glamorgan, one at Merthyr Mawr and the other at Kenfig. Kenfig, now a local nature reserve, includes Kenfig Pool. This pool supports growths of the aquatic Shoreweed in the shallow water and reeds around the margins where Reed Warblers nest in the summer. Mute Swan, Coot and Moorhen are residents on the Pool and in winter they are joined by a large variety of birds, among which are Snipe, Great Crested Grebe, Redshank, Pochard, Teal, Mallard, Tufted Duck, Goldeneye, Bewick's and Whooper Swans, and Cormorants. Grey Herons visit the Pool and a Purple Heron was seen recently as a passage migrant.

The plants of Kenfig Dunes have much in common with those on the Gower dunes. At Kenfig there are extensive areas of dune slacks (wet hollows) along the path to the shore. In the slacks may be found a variety of orchids, particularly Marsh Orchid and Fen Orchid. Both the dune slacks and Kenfig Pool provide breeding sites for Common Frogs and Toads and Crested and Smooth Newts. Common Lizards are found on drier ground and Rabbits and Hares graze on the plants. Predatory birds such as Kestrels, Short-eared Owls, and Buzzards occur at Kenfig while the occasional Peregrine Falcon and Hen Harrier have been recorded here. Bird pellets coughed up by these birds may be found among the dunes.

▲ Wall Pennywort, also known as Navelwort, is abundant on rocks and walls. The tall flower shoots emerge from the foliage in June.

▼ Bewick's Swan is a winter visitor from the Arctic, seen mainly in coastal areas. It feeds on aquatic plants, seeds and grasses.

▲ Kenfig Pool is a large shallow pool at the back of the Kenfig dunes. The pool and the nearby dune slacks form a rich wetland habitat.

▼ Male Smooth Newt in the breeding season. The adults go to water to breed and their future survival depends on the preservation of pools.

Anglesey

Compared with Snowdonia, across the Menai Strait, the scenery of Anglesey is gentle. Its geology is nonetheless varied with contrasting rocks and with tall sea cliffs on the north-west corner near Holyhead. The South Stack Cliffs Reserve in this area is best visited from May to July. Noted primarily for sea birds and wild flowers, it is also frequented by Ravens, Carrion Crows, Choughs, Jackdaws, Stock Doves, and Rock Pipits. Separated from the cliffs are a number of sea stacks, which are particularly attractive to birds that nest on ledges – Guillemots, Razorbills, Puffins, Fulmars, and Herring Gulls. The nesting sites of Razorbills may be spotted by the conspicuous streaks of white guano (bird lime) on the rocks below.

The Blackthorn and other bushes on the heath behind the cliffs attract many small birds such as Wrens, Stonechats, Linnets, and Whitethroats, while some migrants also rest here. Plants of the cliffs are species that are tolerant of salt spray and typical of coastal habitats. They include Thrift, Common Scurvy-grass, English Stonecrop, Wild Thyme, Kidney Vetch, and Wild Carrot. The Marsh Fritillary is one of the numerous butterflies that frequent the cliffs.

A different range of plants grows on the heathland (both wet and dry): Cross-leaved Heath, Bog Asphodel, Bog Pimpernel, Wavy Hair-grass and Tormentil.

Another important but contrasting coastal area is Newborough Warren, which consists of coniferous forest, salt-marshes, and a system of sand dunes that formed in the fourteenth century. The Marram Grass that grows on these dunes was once used by local people to make ropes, matting and baskets.

Malltraeth Pool in the Cefni estuary is a feeding ground for waders and wildfowl. Shelduck, Curlew, Redshank, Pintail, Goldeneye, Whooper and Bewick's Swans, Black-tailed and Bar-tailed Godwits, Ruff and Greenshank, have all been recorded at this site. Specialized plants, including Sea Aster, Annual Seablite, Sea Arrow Grass and Cord Grass, colonize the salt-marsh at Cefni.

▲ The Chough still survives in small numbers in Wales although it is rare in the rest of Britain. It nests on cliff ledges or in caves.

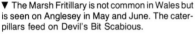

▼ The Marsh Fritillary is not common in Wales but is seen on Anglesey in May and June. The caterpillars feed on Devil's Bit Scabious.

▲ Fulmars breed in colonies on Welsh cliffs in the summer. They lay a single egg on a cliff ledge or in a hollow and do not build a nest.

▼ Thrift, or Sea Pink, grows in dense tufts on coastal cliffs, rocks and the higher parts of salt marshes. The leaves are very narrow.

Cardigan Bay

The long stretch of coastline of Cardigan Bay has fine sandy beaches and therefore attracts many visitors in the summer. In addition to the shore, other areas well worth visiting are the cliff tops around Llangrannog, which are good places to look for flowers, and the Dovey estuary, an excellent spot for birdwatching. Since many of the sandy beaches are exposed and there are few of the rocky shores that harbour more seashore life, the marine life of this area is limited. Seashells are washed up on the shore in a few places, and Topshells, Winkles, Limpets, Dog Whelks and seaweeds are sometimes found on stable boulders.

Inland are the Cambrian Mountains and the smaller Plynlimon Range; here the acid soils support the typical vegetation of mountain moorlands. At the foot of the Cambrian Mountains in the south is Tregaron Bog, a National Nature Reserve. The Welsh name *Cors Goch Glan Teifi* means "the red bog on the banks of the Teifi" and the red colour comes from the sedges and other bog vegetation in autumn.

Tregaron Bog is a classic site as it is a good example of a raised bog. The bog was formed on the bed of a lake of Ice Age origin that was steadily filled in by vegetation. Layers of peat from the reed swamp and later Sphagnum Moss steadily built up to raise the level of the ground. The west bog at Tregaron has suffered little from peat-cutting and is therefore of value as an undisturbed site.

Bog habitats are easily affected by trampling and for this reason access to the bog is limited by permit from the Warden or the Nature Conservancy Council. However, the bird life of the site can be seen from the road which runs alongside. Mammals on Tregaron Reserve include Otters, Water Voles and Polecats.

Further north and on the coast, the Dovey estuary provides a wide range of contrasting habitats. Wetland sites on the Dovey include tidal saltmarshes and also a freshwater marsh known as Borth Bog. On the southern shore of the estuary, at Ynyslas, is a sand dune system with Marram Grass and typical dune flowers.

▲ Spring Squill occurs in dry grassy places, especially near the sea. It grows from a bulb and its star-like flowers can be seen in spring.

▼ Bogbean is a typical plant of bogs and shallow water. It is a near relative of the Gentians and flowers from May to July.

▲ The Otter is an expert swimmer; it dives underwater to catch fish and eels. It usually hides by day and hunts at night.

▼ White-fronted Geese spend the winter in fields, estuaries and marshes on the west coast of Wales; some may occur at Tregaron Bog.

Specialities and Rare Species

Although many of the plants and animals of Wales are widely distributed and occur throughout much of Britain, there are some that are found only in Wales and are therefore of national importance. Yellow Whitlow-grass, for example, grows only on Gower while the red-berried shrub, *Cotoneaster intergerrimus,* grows only on limestone near Llandudno. Other species restricted to Wales are Rock Cinquefoil, three species of Whitebeam, the Skomer Vole, and two freshwater fish, the Gwyniad and a sub- species of Char. Among the birds, the Red Kite survives in mid-Wales but is now extinct in other areas of Britain.

Sea Stock and Hoary Stock, both found in South Wales, are rare flowers that have a limited distribution elsewhere in northwestern Europe. In addition there is a Welsh variety of Common Polypody Fern, which differs considerably in appearance from the more widespread form.

The Freshwater Pearl Mussel lives in soft waters of mountain rivers and streams.

Once more widespread and plentiful, it is now an endangered species in Britain. During the last century this mussel was collected commercially for pearls in both North and South Wales. In the Conwy Valley, entire families lived off the proceeds from pearl fishing. Although the fishing must have depleted the stocks, pollution may also have been responsible for the decline of the species.

Badgers, Weasels and Stoats are common in Wales, as they are in other parts of Britain, but a few other mammals which were once numerous are now rare or have disappeared altogether. Hunting and competition with domestic animals have drastically reduced the native Red and Roe Deer populations and these are now found only in small groups in parks. The Wild Cat has completely disappeared although it once lived in upland regions of Wales. The few remaining feral Goats are mainly restricted to the high mountain crags of North Wales.

▲ The Peregrine Falcon is rare in Wales due largely to the effects of pesticide poisoning.

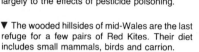

▼ The wooded hillsides of mid-Wales are the last refuge for a few pairs of Red Kites. Their diet includes small mammals, birds and carrion.

▲ The Rock Cinquefoil is very rare. It grows on rocky slopes and flowers in May and June.

▼ Skomer Voles are a sub-species unique to the island of Skomer. They are larger and a lighter colour than Bank Voles on the Welsh mainland

Common Species of the Countryside and Seashore

Some of Britain's animals and plants can be found only in certain regions, or are more easily found in some areas than in others. Living alongside these rare or local species are, of course, many animals and plants which are fairly widespread throughout the country. The more common species of British birds, wild flowers, trees, butterflies, mammals and seashore animals are illustrated on the following pages. These illustrations form a basic field guide to the majority of the regions in Britain.

The captions to the bird illustrations indicate the bird's usual haunts, and if it is seen only in certain seasons, this fact is mentioned. Measurements indicate the size of the bird from the tip of the beak to the end of the tail. Notes to aid identification of the species are also included.

The mammals that are illustrated are accompanied by captions which indicate their average size. Those for hoofed mammals indicate their height at the shoulder. Others indicate the length of their bodies from nose to rump. The captions also give an indication as to when the animal is most active and therefore most easily observed.

The wild flowers are grouped according to their commonest colours; their most frequently used names are given in the captions, along with their habitats, the months in which they flower and their height or the length of creeping stems if they grow horizontally.

The illustrations of butterflies frequently show them on the plants they prefer to visit. The captions indicate the butterflies' usual habitats, the months when they are most frequently seen, and their wingspan.

Information about the sizes of the seashore animals are detailed in their captions, while the height of the trees is given on page 96. Selected identifying characteristics are given in the captions to the trees.

A hedgerow in early summer—one of the countryside's most rewarding habitats, since it shelters a wide variety of species. This illustration features some of the common, widespread plants and animals included in the following pages.

Birds

Canada Goose ▶
Fields and marshes near water; parks. Brown wings and body. Introduced from Canada. 95 cm.

Shag ▶
Rocky coats, where it nests in colonies. Has crest only in breeding season. Flies low, close to the water. 78 cm.

Cormorant ▶
Near the sea and some large inland waters. Has white thigh patch in breeding season. Larger than Shag. 92 cm.

Spring

◀ Mute Swan
Wide rivers, lakes, town parks. Not, as its name implies, mute. Britain's most common swan. 152 cm.

▼ Wigeon
Near sea, especially in winter, lakes and marshes. Seen August-April; a few stay to breed. 46 cm.

Mallard ▲
Inland waters and estuaries. Purplish-blue wing patch seen in flight. 58 cm.

◀ Pintail
Lakes and marshes, near coast in winter. Pointed tail and long, elegant neck. Seen September-March; a few stay to breed. 66 cm.

Shoveler ▶
Quiet lakes and shallow water. Large, heavy bill. Pale blue forewings of both male and female show in flight. 51 cm.

▼ Teal
Inland waters and estuaries. The smallest duck in Britain. Dark bill. Quick and agile in flight. 35 cm.

▲ Tufted Duck
Lakes, ponds, gravel pits and parks. Dumpy, active diving duck. Note female's yellow eye. 43 cm.

36

▼ Pochard
Lakes and backwaters. In flight, both sexes have dark wings with paler grey central bar. 46 cm.

▲ Shelduck
Coasts and estuaries, often in flocks; also large inland lakes. Female has no red knob on bill. 61 cm.

▲ Red-breasted Merganser
Coastal areas; wooded lakes, rivers, in breeding season. 58 cm.

Grey Heron ▶
Near water: rivers, lakes and seashores. Head is drawn back in flight. 92 cm.

Summer

Winter

▼ Little Grebe
Inland waters. Secretive and hard to spot. 27 cm.

▲ Great Crested Grebe
Inland waters, sometimes on sea in winter. 48 cm.

Winter

Summer

Buzzard ▼
Often seen soaring over moors
and farmland. Rare in east and
south-east England. 54 cm.

▼ Kestrel
Moors, coasts, farmland;
some nest in towns.
Hovers when hunting.
34 cm.

Coot ►
Lakes, reservoirs,
open water.
Larger, heavier
bird than
Moorhen.
38 cm.

▲ Moorhen
Ponds, lakes and streams. 33 cm.

◄ Partridge
Farmland, moors. Small head,
short tail and legs. Often in
small groups. 30 cm.

♂

▼ Pheasant
Farmland, scrub,
woodland. Males can
have white neckring.
Male 87 cm, female
58 cm.

♀

38

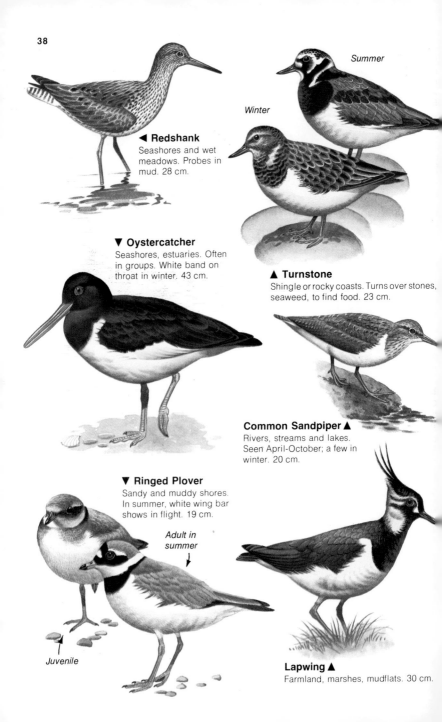

Summer

Winter

◄ Redshank
Seashores and wet
meadows. Probes in
mud. 28 cm.

▼ Oystercatcher
Seashores, estuaries. Often
in groups. White band on
throat in winter. 43 cm.

▲ Turnstone
Shingle or rocky coasts. Turns over stones,
seaweed, to find food. 23 cm.

Common Sandpiper ▲
Rivers, streams and lakes.
Seen April-October; a few in
winter. 20 cm.

▼ Ringed Plover
Sandy and muddy shores.
In summer, white wing bar
shows in flight. 19 cm.

*Adult in
summer*

Juvenile

Lapwing ▲
Farmland, marshes, mudflats. 30 cm.

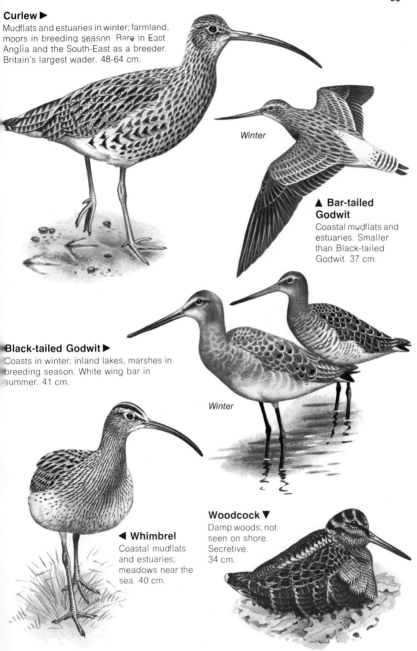

Curlew ▶
Mudflats and estuaries in winter; farmland,
moors in breeding season. Rare in East
Anglia and the South-East as a breeder.
Britain's largest wader. 48-64 cm.

Winter

**▲ Bar-tailed
Godwit**
Coastal mudflats and
estuaries. Smaller
than Black-tailed
Godwit. 37 cm.

Black-tailed Godwit ▶
Coasts in winter; inland lakes, marshes in
breeding season. White wing bar in
summer. 41 cm.

Winter

◀ Whimbrel
Coastal mudflats
and estuaries;
meadows near the
sea. 40 cm.

Woodcock ▼
Damp woods; not
seen on shore.
Secretive.
34 cm.

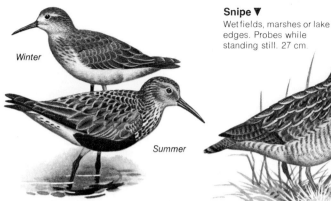

Winter

Summer

▲ Dunlin
Mudflats and estuaries. Common winter shorebird; less common in summer. 19 cm.

Snipe ▼
Wet fields, marshes or lake edges. Probes while standing still. 27 cm.

Winter

▲ Sanderling
Sandy shores along coasts. Seen August-May. Short, straight beak. 20 cm.

Greenshank ▼
Coasts, marshes. Seen chiefly on migration. Some breed in Scotland. 30 cm.

Summer

♂

◄ Ruff
Marshes, wet meadows, edges of reservoirs. Seen mostly in spring and autumn. 29 cm.

♂

▼ Knot
Sand or mudflats in estuaries. Larger tha Dunlin. Seen mostly August-May. 25 cm.

Winter

Winter

▼ Common Tern
Near sea; also nests inland in Scotland.
Seen April-October. 34 cm.

Summer

◀ Little Tern
Shingle beaches. Never
has full black cap like other
terns. Seen
April-September. 24 cm.

Summer

Herring Gull ▼
Coastal ports and seaside
towns. Wingtips are black
with white spots. 56 cm.

◀ Black-headed Gull
Inland and near the sea. Dark
brown "hood" in summer
only. 37 cm.

Summer

Summer

Common Gull ▶
Coasts; often inland in
winter. Smaller and
less widespread than
Herring Gull. 41 cm.

Lesser Black-backed Gull ▶
Coasts and inland.
Mainly a summer
visitor. 53 cm.

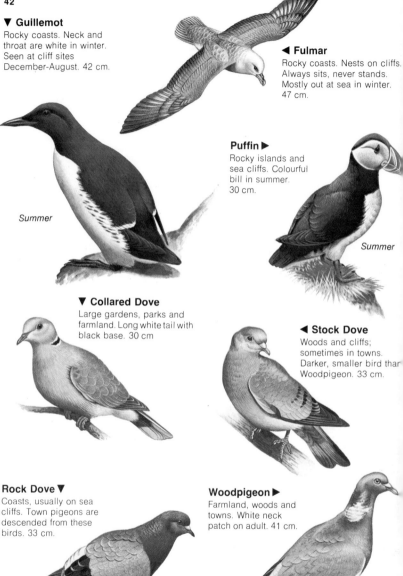

▼ Guillemot
Rocky coasts. Neck and
throat are white in winter.
Seen at cliff sites
December-August. 42 cm.

◄ Fulmar
Rocky coasts. Nests on cliffs.
Always sits, never stands.
Mostly out at sea in winter.
47 cm.

Puffin ►
Rocky islands and
sea cliffs. Colourful
bill in summer.
30 cm.

Summer

Summer

▼ Collared Dove
Large gardens, parks and
farmland. Long white tail with
black base. 30 cm

◄ Stock Dove
Woods and cliffs;
sometimes in towns.
Darker, smaller bird than
Woodpigeon. 33 cm.

Rock Dove ▼
Coasts, usually on sea
cliffs. Town pigeons are
descended from these
birds. 33 cm.

Woodpigeon ►
Farmland, woods and
towns. White neck
patch on adult. 41 cm.

▼ Short-eared Owl
Open country. Hunts in
day-time or at dusk. 37 cm.

◄ Barn Owl
Open country,
especially
farmland. Mostly
nocturnal. 34 cm.

**◄ Long-eared
Owl**
Edges of woods.
Underside all dark.
Nocturnal. 34 cm.

Little Owl ▼
Farmland and wooded
country. Underside is
streaked. Often seen in
daylight. 22 cm.

▲ Tawny Owl
Parks, woodland and
farmland; sometimes towns.
Large head. Nocturnal. 38 cm.

◄ Kingfisher
Near rivers and
lakes; seashore in
winter. Dives from
low perch or from a
hover. 17 cm.

▼ Cuckoo
Anywhere in countryside.
Male's song is well known.
April-September. 30 cm.

Swift ▶
Breeds mainly in towns; may fly over countryside. Seen end of April-August/September. 17 cm.

▼ Sand Martin
Banks and sandy cliffs. Seen April-September. 12 cm.

◀ House Martin
Suburban areas and countryside. Seen April-October. 13 cm.

◀ Swallow
Farms and open country often near water. Seen April-September/October. 19 cm.

◀ Great Spotted Woodpecker
Woodlands. Large white patches on wings. 23 cm.

◀ Green Woodpecker
Deciduous woods, parks. Yellow-green rump seen in flight. Rare in Scotland. 32 cm.

Lesser Spotted Woodpecker ▶
Deciduous woods, parks. Not in Scotland. Sparrow-sized. 14 cm.

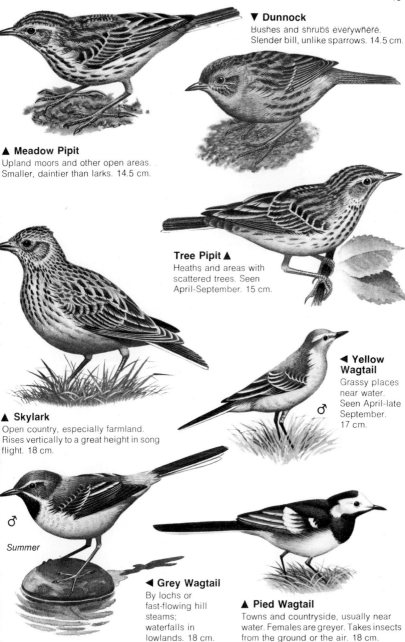

▼ Dunnock
Bushes and shrubs everywhere.
Slender bill, unlike sparrows. 14.5 cm.

▲ Meadow Pipit
Upland moors and other open areas.
Smaller, daintier than larks. 14.5 cm.

Tree Pipit ▲
Heaths and areas with
scattered trees. Seen
April-September. 15 cm.

**◄ Yellow
Wagtail**
Grassy places
near water.
Seen April-late
September.
17 cm.

♂

▲ Skylark
Open country, especially farmland.
Rises vertically to a great height in song
flight. 18 cm.

♂

Summer

◄ Grey Wagtail
By lochs or
fast-flowing hill
steams;
waterfalls in
lowlands. 18 cm.

▲ Pied Wagtail
Towns and countryside, usually near
water. Females are greyer. Takes insects
from the ground or the air. 18 cm.

▼ Willow Warbler
Gardens, woods and hedgerows. Flatter head and longer tail than Chiffchaff. Seen April-September. 11 cm.

▲ Sedge Warbler
Thick vegetation near water. Broad, pale stripe over eye. Seen April-September. 13 cm.

Wren ▶
Towns and countryside. Tiny, rotund bird with cocked tail. 9.5 cm.

Reed Warbler ▼
Reed beds. Not in Scotland. Seen April-September. 13 cm.

♂

♀

▲ Blackcap
Wooded areas. Seen April-September, a few in winter. 14 cm.

▼ Whitethroat
Thick, low bushes. Seen April-September. 14 cm.

▲ Garden Warbler
Hedges or woods with thick undergrowth. Seen April-September. 14 cm.

Chiffchaff ▼
Woods and copses.
Seen March-September;
a few in winter. 11 cm.

▲ Wood Warbler
Open woods with
sparse undergrowth.
Seen April-August.
13 cm.

♂

♀

Wheatear ▼
Open country, especially
moors and downs. Seen
March-October. 15 cm.

♂

▲ Whinchat
Rough grassland, moors with
scrub, bracken, etc. Seen
April-September. 13 cm.

◄ Pied Flycatcher
Deciduous woods, especially
oak. Seen April-September.
13 cm.

♀

Spotted Flycatcher ▶
Parks, gardens, open
woods. Seen
May-September.
14 cm.

48

Blackbird ▼
In trees and bushes everywhere. Young are paler than female with breast more strongly spotted. 25 cm.

▼ Starling
Most places, including cities. In summer, has purple and green gloss and mostly yellow bill. 22 cm.

Juvenile

Adult in winter

▲ Redwing
Farmland, commons and other open areas. A few breed in Scotland. Seen October-April. 21 cm.

◄ Fieldfare
Farmland, orchards, open areas. White underwings. Seen October-April. 25.5 cm.

▼ Redstart
Heaths, parks, open woods. Seen April-September. Rather Robin-like. 14 cm.

Robin ▲
Gardens, hedgerows and woodland. Juvenile is spotted, without any red. 14 cm.

◄ Song Thrush
Trees and bushes in towns and country.
Smashes snails on stones. 23 cm.

Long-tailed Tit ►
Hedgerows and
woodland edges.
14 cm. (7.5 cm of
which is the tail).

◄ Great Tit
Gardens and
woodlands. Black
band on chest. 14 cm.

◄ Blue Tit
Woods and gardens.
Dark line on belly.
11 cm.

▲ Mistle Thrush
Woodland and open areas.
Larger than Blackbird: paler,
greyer than Song Thrush. 27 cm.

▼ Marsh Tit
Deciduous woods;
infrequently in
gardens. 11 cm.

▲ Coal Tit
Coniferous woods, parks,
gardens. Oblong white patch
on nape. 11 cm.

50

▼ Chaffinch
Farmland, hedgerows and
woodland. Male is duller in winter.
White wing bar seen in flight.
15 cm.

♀

♂

Summer

▲ Siskin
Usually coniferous woods in
summer; birch, alder woods,
sometimes gardens, in winter. 11 cm.

▲ Nuthatch
Deciduous wood and parks. Can
descend trees head-first. Very
short tail. Rare in Scotland.
14 cm.

▲ Hawfinch
Deciduous woodland,
orchards. Very elusive. Big
head and massive, broad
bill. 16 cm.

◄ Treecreeper
Woodland, sometimes parks
and gardens. Creeps up tree
trunks using tail as support. 13 cm.

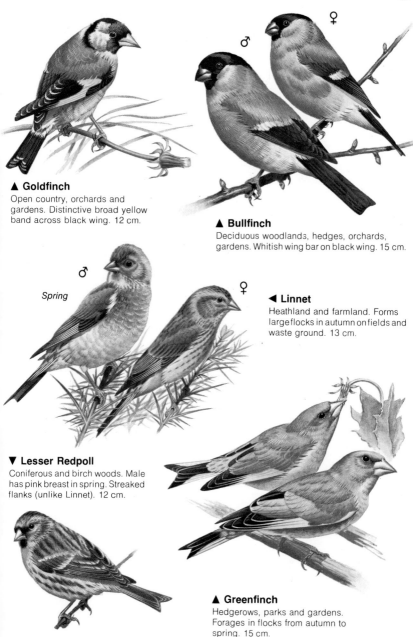

▲ Goldfinch
Open country, orchards and gardens. Distinctive broad yellow band across black wing. 12 cm.

▲ Bullfinch
Deciduous woodlands, hedges, orchards, gardens. Whitish wing bar on black wing. 15 cm.

Spring

◀ Linnet
Heathland and farmland. Forms large flocks in autumn on fields and waste ground. 13 cm.

▼ Lesser Redpoll
Coniferous and birch woods. Male has pink breast in spring. Streaked flanks (unlike Linnet). 12 cm.

▲ Greenfinch
Hedgerows, parks and gardens. Forages in flocks from autumn to spring. 15 cm.

▼ Tree Sparrow
Farmland. White cheeks with black spot. Sometimes flocks with House Sparrow in winter. 14 cm.

▲ House Sparrow
Near houses in cities; on farms in the country. Distinctive black bib on male. 15 cm.

▲ Corn Bunting
Open country, especially cornfields. Bigger than other buntings and finches. 18 cm.

▲ Yellowhammer
Farmland, heaths, young plantations. Flocks forage in fields in winter. Rare in Wales. 17 cm.

▲ Goldcrest
Large gardens and woods, especially conifers. Smallest British bird. 9 cm.

▲ Reed Bunting
Vegetation near water; may visit bird tables in winter. Male has less black on head in winter. 15 cm.

Carrion Crow ▶
Open country, town, along coasts. Usually seen alone, in pairs or small groups. 47 cm.

▼ Jay
Woodlands, parks and gardens. White rump and blue wing flash show in flight. 32 cm.

◀ Magpie
Hedgerows, farmland, scrub. Large black and white bird. Long, slender tail. 46 cm.

▼ Jackdaw
Cliffs, farmland and towns. Small black and grey crow. Forms large flocks. 33 cm.

▲ Rook
Farmland, open copses, villages. Forms large flocks. Baggy thighs. Bare whitish face in adults. 46 cm.

Mammals

▼ Red Fox
Farmland and woods, sometimes mountains and towns. Mainly nocturnal. 65 cm.

▲ Badger
Woods, sometimes mountains. Nocturnal. Can stay underground for several days in cold weather without food. 80 cm.

▼ Roe Deer
Conifer plantations, especially near water. Mainly nocturnal; hides during day. 70 cm.

▲ Hedgehog
Hedgerows, ditches, parks, gardens and moorland. Mainly nocturnal. 25 cm. .

▲ Mole
Underground in most kinds of soil in farmland, woods. Lives alone. Can swim well. 13 cm.

▼ Grey Squirrel
Woods, parks and gardens.
Introduced from N. America.
Diurnal. 27 cm.

Red Squirrel ▲
Mainly conifer woods. Partly replaced
by Grey Squirrel in England. 23 cm.

▼ Rabbit
Farmland, woodland, sand
dunes and hillsides. Active
at dusk and dawn. 40 cm.

◄ Brown Hare
Open farmland and
woodland. Mainly
nocturnal, but can often be
seen in day. 58 cm.

▼ Wood Mouse
Gardens,
hedgerows,
woods. Mainly
nocturnal. 9 cm.

▼ Common Shrew
Rough pasture, woods,
hedgerows, dunes and
marshes. Active day and
night. 7 cm.

▼ Short-tailed Vole
Open ground with
rough grass. Most
active at night; also
seen in day. 11 cm.

◀ Grey Seal
Rocky shores, mainly along Atlantic coast; some on east coast of Scotland and north-east coast of England. 3 m.

Common Seal ▶
Flat shores, estuaries and mudbanks on Scottish coasts and mainly east coast of England. Blunter head than Grey Seal. 1.5 m.

 ◀ Stoat
Woods, farmland, mountains. Tip of tail always black. Mainly nocturnal. 28 cm.

▲ Weasel
Same habitat as Stoat, but prefers dry places. Mainly nocturnal. 20 cm.

Water Vole ▶
Ponds, canals, streams and marshes. Mainly diurnal. May also be black. 19 cm.

Otter ▶
Alongside rivers, lakes; marshes, coasts and the sea. Nocturnal. More common in Scotland. 70 cm.

Wild Flowers

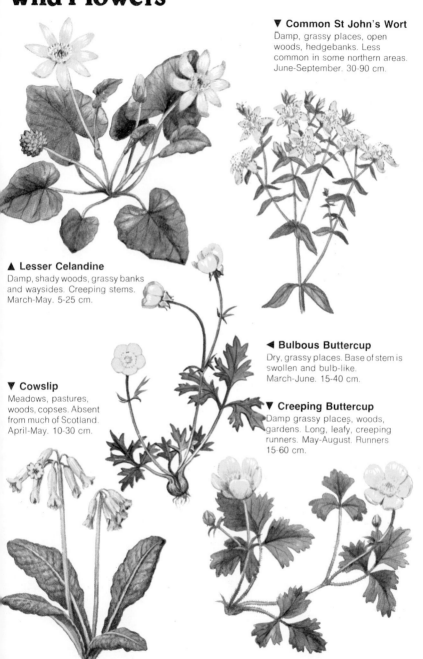

▼ **Common St John's Wort**
Damp, grassy places, open
woods, hedgebanks. Less
common in some northern areas.
June-September. 30-90 cm.

▲ **Lesser Celandine**
Damp, shady woods, grassy banks
and waysides. Creeping stems.
March-May. 5-25 cm.

◄ **Bulbous Buttercup**
Dry, grassy places. Base of stem is
swollen and bulb-like.
March-June. 15-40 cm.

▼ **Cowslip**
Meadows, pastures,
woods, copses. Absent
from much of Scotland.
April-May. 10-30 cm.

▼ **Creeping Buttercup**
Damp grassy places, woods,
gardens. Long, leafy, creeping
runners. May-August. Runners
15-60 cm.

▼ Creeping Jenny
Grassy, shady places; damp meadows, woods, under hedges. Rare in northern Scotland. June-August. Stems up to 60 cm.

◀ Yellow Rattle
Waysides and other grassy places. Seeds rattle inside ripe capsule. May-August. 12-40 cm.

Common Rockrose ▶
Grassy, rocky places. Not a rose. Leaves are hairy. May-September 5-30 cm.

Aaron's Rod ▶
Banks, waste places, open scrub. Rarer in Scotland. June-August. 30-200 cm.

◄ Groundsel
Waste places; a
common garden weed.
Flowers all year round.
8-45 cm.

▲ Primrose
Woods, hedges and fields. Rarer
in the North. February-May.
8-15 cm.

◄ Herb Bennet
Woods, hedges, shady places.
Fruits are hooked. June-August.
20-60 cm.

◄ Broom
Heaths, waste ground,
open woods,
scrubland. May-June.
60-200 cm.

▲ Yellow Pimpernel
Woods and shady
hedgebanks. May-September.
Trailing stems up to 40 cm long.

60

◀ Silverweed
Hedgebanks, grassy
places. Creeping stems.
May-August.

*Fruits
(in autumn)*

▲ Old Man's Beard
Woodland edges, hedgerows, scrub.
Rare in Scotland and northern
England. July-August. Up to 30 m.

▼ Bird's Foot Trefoil
Open, grassy places. Very long,
creeping stems. Pods look like a
bird's foot. May-June.

Golden Rod ▶
Woods, cliffs, hedges. Rarer
in the South-East.
July-September. 5-75 cm.

**▼ Creeping
Cinquefoil**
Hedgebanks, grassy
places. Creeping
stems. May-August.

▼ Ragwort

Roadsides, waste ground, grassy places. Flowerheads in flat-topped clusters. June-October. 30-150 cm

▲ Dandelion

Open grassy places and waste ground. March-October. 15-30 cm.

Rape ▶

Roadsides and fields. May-August. Up to 1m.

▼ Gorse

Heaths and commons. March-July. 60-200 cm.

▲ Wild Pansy

Grassy places and cornfields. Flowers can also be all yellow, all violet, or pink and white. April-September. 15-45 cm.

▼ Viper's Bugloss
Waysides and sand dunes. Sharp hairs on stems. Bristly leaves. Rare in Scotland. June-September. 30-90 cm.

Common Forget-me-Not ▶
Roadsides, fields, and open grassy places. April-September. 15-30 cm.

◀ Sea Aster
Saltmarshes. Petals can also be white. July-October. 1 m.

◀ Common Speedwell
Grassy places and woods. May-August. 10-40 cm.

Common Milkwort ▶
Heaths, dunes, grassy places. May-September. 10-30 cm.

▼ Brooklime

In and by ponds, streams and other wet places. May-September. 20-60 cm.

Lesser Periwinkle ▶

Woods and hedgebanks. March-May. Flowering stems up to 15 cm.

Harebell ▼

Dry grasslands and heaths. Called Bluebell in Scotland. Locally common throughout Britain. July-August. 15-40 cm.

Bugle ▶

Damp woods and grassy places. Has creeping runners. Leaves are often purplish. May-July. 10-30 cm.

▲ Bluebell

Woods and hedgebanks. Flowers can also be white or pink. April-June. 20-50 cm.

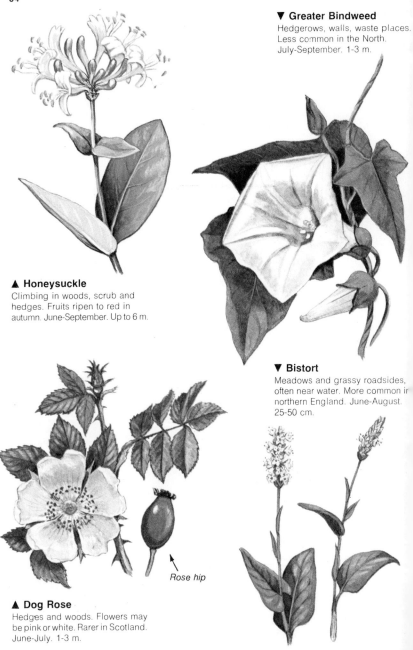

▼ Greater Bindweed
Hedgerows, walls, waste places.
Less common in the North.
July-September. 1-3 m.

▲ Honeysuckle
Climbing in woods, scrub and
hedges. Fruits ripen to red in
autumn. June-September. Up to 6 m.

▼ Bistort
Meadows and grassy roadsides,
often near water. More common in
northern England. June-August.
25-50 cm.

Rose hip

▲ Dog Rose
Hedges and woods. Flowers may
be pink or white. Rarer in Scotland.
June-July. 1-3 m.

▼ **Knotgrass**
Waste ground, fields and
seashores. A low, far-spreading
plant, July-October. Creeping
stems 3-200 cm.

Great Willowherb ▶
Ditches, marshes, near
streams. Rare in
northern Scotland.
July-August. 80-150 cm.

◀ **Sea Bindweed**
Sandy beaches;
sometimes shingle.
Rare in Scotland.
June-August. Trailing
stems up to
50 cm.

▼ **Sand Spurrey**
Sandy or gravelly places. Leaves
end in a small bristle.
May-September.
5-25 cm.

▲ **Sea Milkwort**
Grassy saltmarshes.
Creeping stems.
June-August.
10-30 cm tall.

◀ **Thrift**
Rocky cliffs near coast;
mountains inland.
March-October.
5-30 cm.

66

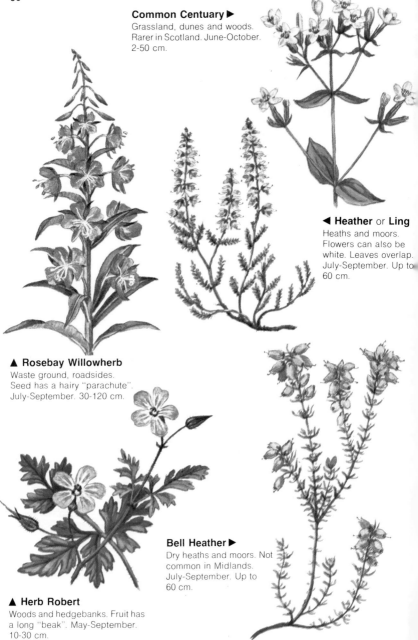

Common Centuary ▶
Grassland, dunes and woods.
Rarer in Scotland. June-October.
2-50 cm.

◀ Heather or **Ling**
Heaths and moors.
Flowers can also be
white. Leaves overlap.
July-September. Up to
60 cm.

▲ Rosebay Willowherb
Waste ground, roadsides.
Seed has a hairy "parachute".
July-September. 30-120 cm.

Bell Heather ▶
Dry heaths and moors. Not
common in Midlands.
July-September. Up to
60 cm.

▲ Herb Robert
Woods and hedgebanks. Fruit has
a long "beak". May-September.
10-30 cm.

▼ Bilberry

Heaths, moors and woods.
Blue-black berries. Flowers
April-June. Up to 60 cm.

Ragged Robin ▲

Damp meadows,
marshes, woods. Sepals
form a tube. May-June.
30-75 cm.

Lady's Smock ▼

Damp meadows and near streams.
Flower can be pink or white and
lilac. April-June. 15-60 cm.

▲ Lesser Knapweed

Grassland and waysides. Stem is
grooved below flowerhead.
June-September. 15-60 cm.

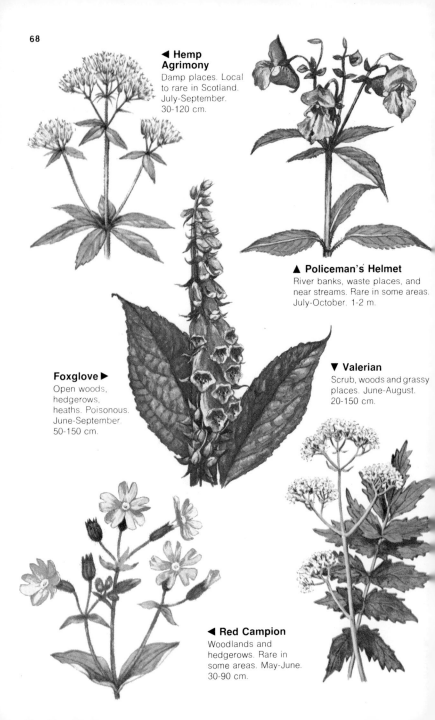

68

◄ Hemp Agrimony
Damp places. Local to rare in Scotland. July-September. 30-120 cm.

▲ Policeman's Helmet
River banks, waste places, and near streams. Rare in some areas. July-October. 1-2 m.

Foxglove ►
Open woods, hedgerows, heaths. Poisonous. June-September. 50-150 cm.

▼ Valerian
Scrub, woods and grassy places. June-August. 20-150 cm.

◄ Red Campion
Woodlands and hedgerows. Rare in some areas. May-June. 30-90 cm.

◀ **Watermint**
Near water, marshes,
damp woods.
July-October. 15-90 cm.

**Early Purple
Orchid** ▶
Woods and copses.
Locally common
throughout Britain.
May-June. 15-60 cm.

◀ **Devil's Bit
Scabious**
Wet grassy places.
June-October.
15-100 cm.

◀ **Wild Teasel**
Roadsides, woodland
edges, near streams.
July-August. 50-200 cm.

**Common Dog
Violet** ▶
Hedgerows and
woods.
April-July.
5-20 cm.

▲ **Field Scabious**
Dry grassland, waste
places. June-
September. 15-80 cm.

Tufted Vetch ▼
Climbs on other plants in hedges
and grassy places. June-August.
Flowers 10 mm long.

▲ Ivy-leaved Toadflax
Old walls, occasionally rocks.
Often forms clumps. May-September.
Flowers 10 mm long.

Sea Lavender ▼
Muddy saltmarshes. Often forms
large mats. Not in northern
Scotland. July-October. 8-30 cm.

▲ Woody Nightshade
Hedges, woods, waste places. Poisonous.
Not common in Scotland. June-September.
Scrambling stems 30-200 cm.

▼ Long-headed Poppy
Corn and other fields and waste ground.
Longer capsule and paler petals than
Field Poppy. June-July. 20-60 cm.

Capsule

▲ Scarlet Pimpernel
Cultivated and waste ground. A
sub-species has small blue flowers.
Rarer in Scotland. June-August.
6-30 cm.

◄ Field Poppy
Corn and other fields,
waste ground. Rare in
northern Scotland.
June-August. 20-60 cm.

Capsule

**▼ Wood
Woundwort**
Woods, hedgebanks,
waste ground.
July-August.
30-100 cm.

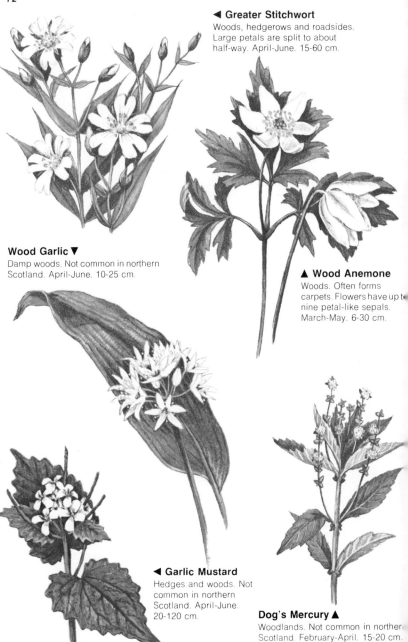

◄ Greater Stitchwort
Woods, hedgerows and roadsides.
Large petals are split to about
half-way. April-June. 15-60 cm.

Wood Garlic ▼
Damp woods. Not common in northern
Scotland. April-June. 10-25 cm.

▲ Wood Anemone
Woods. Often forms
carpets. Flowers have up to
nine petal-like sepals.
March-May. 6-30 cm.

◄ Garlic Mustard
Hedges and woods. Not
common in northern
Scotland. April-June.
20-120 cm.

Dog's Mercury ▲
Woodlands. Not common in northern
Scotland. February-April. 15-20 cm.

▼ White Bryony
Climbs in hedges and scrub.
Berries are poisonous. Rarer
in Scotland. May-September.
Up to 4 m.

▼ Wild Strawberry
Woods and scrubland. Leaves
have three leaflets. Can cover
large patches. April-July.

Cow Parsley ▼
Hedgebanks, roadsides, ditches.
Leaves are divided into feathery
segments. April-June. 60-100 cm.

▼ Upright Hedge Parsley
Roadsides, grassy places.
Flowers later than Cow Parsley,
and leaves less feathery.
July-August. 50-125 cm.

▼ **Meadowsweet**
Marshes, water meadows and near
ditches. Flowers smell sweet.
May-September 60-120 cm.

▲ **Water Crowfoot**
Ponds, streams and
ditches. May-June.
Flowers are 10-20 mm
across.

Wild Carrot ▶
Grassy places, especially near
the sea. June-August. 30-100 cm.

Hogweed ▲
Open woods, roadsides,
grassy places.
June-September.
50-200 cm.

Daisy ▲
Short grassland, especially lawns.
March-October. 3-12 cm.

▼ White Dead Nettle

Roadsides, hedgerows and waste ground. Rare in north Scotland. May-December. 20-60 cm.

▲ Nettle

Waysides, waste ground, woods. Has stinging hairs. June-August. 30-150 cm.

▼ White Clover

Garden lawns, grassy places. June-September. Upright stems up to 25 cm.

▲ Shepherd's Purse

Waysides and waste ground. Flowers all year. 3-40 cm.

◄ White Campion
Waysides, hedgebanks, waste
ground. Sticky hairs. May-September.
30-100 cm.

**◄ Bladder
Campion**
Roadsides and grassy
places. Usually
hairless. June-August.
25-90 cm.

◄ Sea Campion
Sea cliffs, shingle beaches.
Smaller than Bladder Campion
with broader petals.
June-August. 8-25 cm.

▼ Chickweed
Fields, waste places,
gardens. Flowers all year.
5-40 cm.

▲ Corn Spurrey
Cornfields, cultivated
land. June-August.
7-40 cm.

Yarrow ▲
Waste ground and
grassy places. June-
August. 8-45 cm.

▲ Ox-eye Daisy
Grassy places and roadsides.
Upper leaves are toothed.
June-August. 20-70 cm.

Sea Sandwort ▶
Sand and shingle
beaches. May-August.
5-25 cm.

▼ Pellitory-of-the-wall
Wall and rock crevices. Not in
northern Scotland. June-October.
30-100 cm.

▲ Wood Sorrel
Woods and hedgebanks. Flowers
close at night and in bad weather.
Petals have lilac veins. April-May. 5-15 cm.

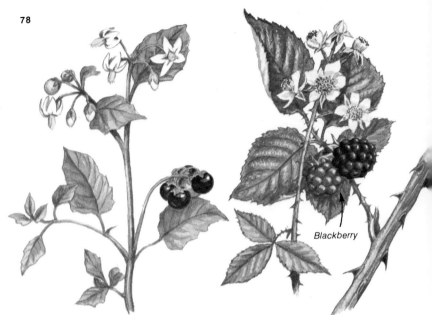

Blackberry

▲ **Black Nightshade**
Cultivated and waste ground. Rare in
Scotland. July-September. Up to 60 cm.

▲ **Bramble**
Woods, scrubland, hedges, open
ground. May-September. Arching
stems up to 5 m.

▼ **Greater Plantain**
Cultivated land, waysides,
lawns. Broad leaves.
May-September. 10-15 cm.

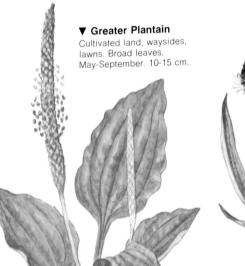

▲ **Ribwort Plantain**
Grassy and waste places, lawns.
Ribbed leaves. April-August.
Up to 45 cm.

Butterflies

♀

▲ Wall Brown
Woodlands and rough, open
ground. Often rests on walls. Not in
northern Scotland. Seen
March-September. 44-46 mm.

Wall Brown ♂

Grayling ♀

♂

▲ Grayling
Sandy places, chalk downs. Less
common in Wales and East Anglia.
Seen July-August. 56-61 mm.

♂

Meadow Brown ♀

▲ Meadow Brown
Meadows and other grassy places.
Less common in Scotland. Seen
June-September. 50-55 mm.

Small Heath ▶
Many areas including open
woods, marshes and dry
hillsides. Seen April-September.
33-35 mm.

80

Painted Lady ▶
Dry, open places. Likes
thistles. Seen
June-October. 62-65 mm.

Painted Lady

Red Admiral ▶
Gardens and woodland edges.
Migrant from North Africa. Seen
May-October. 66-68 mm.

▲ Small Tortoiseshell
Gardens and open places. Less
widespread in Wales and
Scotland. Seen April-November.
48-52 mm.
▼

*Small
Tortoiseshell*

▲ Peacock
Gardens. Not present in northern Scotland.
Seen August-October. 62-68 mm.

▲ **Orange Tip**
Woodland edges and hedgerows. Not in parts of Scotland. Seen April-June. 42-48 mm.
▼

♀

♂

Orange Tip

▲ **Common Blue**
Prefers downs and rough meadows. Seen April-September. 28-36 mm.

♂

Common Blue

♂

▼ **Small Copper**
All types of country. Less widespread in Scotland. Seen May-September. 26-30 mm.

Caterpillar of Small Copper

♂

♀

♀

♂

♂

▲ **Large White**
Woods, gardens and open places. Caterpillar eats brassicas. Seen May-August. 62-64 mm.

Large White ♀

♀

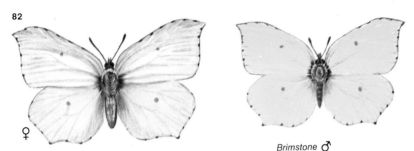

♀

▲ Brimstone
Hedges, gardens and woodland paths.
Adult hibernates. Not in Scotland. Seen
June-September. 58-60 mm.

Brimstone ♂

▼ Small White
Gardens and other cultivated places.
Less widespread in Scotland. Seen
May-August. 48-50 mm.

♀

♀

♂

♂

▼ Green-veined White
Open woodland and grassy places,
gardens. Caterpillar eats leaves and
seed-pods of Garlic Mustard. Seen
May-September. 47-50 mm.

♀

♂

Seashore

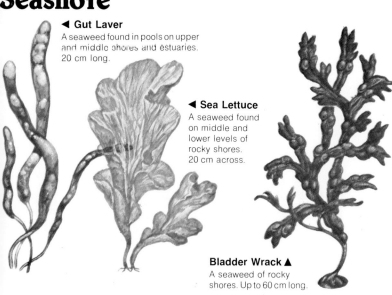

◄ Gut Laver
A seaweed found in pools on upper and middle shores and estuaries. 20 cm long.

◄ Sea Lettuce
A seaweed found on middle and lower levels of rocky shores. 20 cm across.

Bladder Wrack ▲
A seaweed of rocky shores. Up to 60 cm long.

◄ Channelled Wrack
A seaweed found on rocks of the upper shore. 10 cm tall.

▼ Bread-crumb Sponge
On rocks, shells and seaweed holdfasts. 10 cm across.

▲ Haliclona oculata
A sponge found on lower shores in fast currents and estuaries with muddy gravel. Up to 16 cm long.

Sea Oak ►
A seaweed found in pools, on stalks of other seaweeds and on rocks. 20 cm tall.

84

▼ Beadlet Anemone
Rock pools at most levels of the
shore. 5 cm high.

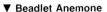

▼ Snakelocks Anemone
Rocky shores. Not on east or south-east
coasts. Can be grey or greenish. 10 cm
across.

▲ Daisy Anemone
In rock crevices or mud of shallow
pools. 10 cm high.

*Dahlia
Anemone*

▲ Dahlia Anemone
In crevices in rock pools. 15 cm
high when open.

◄ Hermit Crab Anemone
On mollusc shells inhabited by
Hermit Crab. 10 cm high.

◄ Common Hermit Crab
Mostly lower shore, in rock pools.
5-10 cm long.

▲ Common Limpet
On rocky shores, attached to rocks. 7 cm long.

▲ Common Periwinkle
On rocky and muddy shores. 2.5 cm high.

▲ Netted Dog Whelk
On mud and gravel off shore and on lower shore. 2.5 cm high.

▲ Saddle Oyster
On lower shore, attached to rocks. 6 cm wide.

▲ Common Whelk
Lower shore of rocky or sandy beaches. 8 cm high.

▲ Slipper Limpet
Low water and off shore, often attached to one another. 4-5 cm long.

▲ Common Mussel
Rocky shores, pier piles and estuaries. 1-10 cm long.

▲ Dog Whelk
On rocks and in crevices of lower shore. 3 cm high.

▲ Painted Topshell
On rocks and under stones on lower shore. 2.5 cm high.

▲ Common Oyster
Shallow and deep water. 10-15 cm long.

▲ Necklace Shell
Sandy shores. 3 cm high.

▲ Rayed Trough Shell
Sand or gravel on lower shores. 5 cm long.

▲ Razor Shell
Burrows in mud. 12 cm long.

▲ Baltic Tellin
In mud and sand of seashores and estuaries.
2 cm long.

▲ Common Sand Gaper
Burrows in muddy sand on lower shore.
12 cm wide.

▲ Horse Mussel
From lower shore to deep water. 20 cm long.

▲ Edible Cockle
In mud and sand of middle shore and below.
4 cm across.

▲ Flat Periwinkle
Under brown seaweed on rocky shores.
1 cm high.

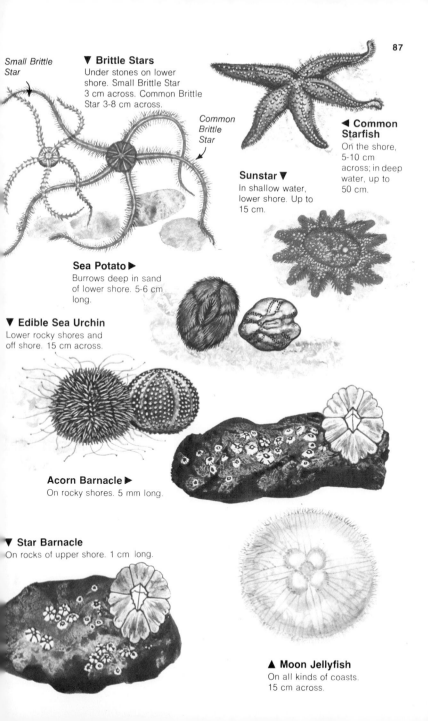

Small Brittle Star

▼ Brittle Stars
Under stones on lower shore. Small Brittle Star 3 cm across. Common Brittle Star 3-8 cm across.

Common Brittle Star

◄ Common Starfish
On the shore, 5-10 cm across; in deep water, up to 50 cm.

Sunstar ▼
In shallow water, lower shore. Up to 15 cm.

Sea Potato ►
Burrows deep in sand of lower shore. 5-6 cm long.

▼ Edible Sea Urchin
Lower rocky shores and off shore. 15 cm across.

Acorn Barnacle ►
On rocky shores. 5 mm long.

▼ Star Barnacle
On rocks of upper shore. 1 cm long.

▲ Moon Jellyfish
On all kinds of coasts. 15 cm across.

88

▲ Common Prawn
Shallow water and rock pools. 5-8 cm long.

▼ Common Lobster
Only small ones in rock pools of lower shore. Can grow up to 45 cm long elsewhere.

▲ White Shrimp
Rock pools on lower shore; shallow waters of estuaries. 5 cm long.

▼ Montagu's Plated Lobster
Under seaweed and stones of lower shore. 4-6 cm long.

▲ Sand Shrimp
Sand estuaries. 5 cm long.

▼ Edible Crab
Only small ones in rock pools in lower shore. Can grow up to 11.5 cm long elsewhere.

▲ Shore Crab
Sandy, muddy and rocky shores; estuaries. 8 cm across.

▲ Broad-clawed Porcelain Crab
Under stones on middle and lower shores. 1.2 cm across.

Cuttlebone

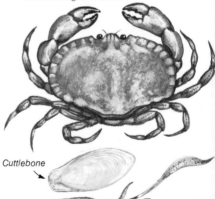

▲ Common Cuttlefish
In sheltered bays and washed up dead on strand line. 30 cm long.

Trees

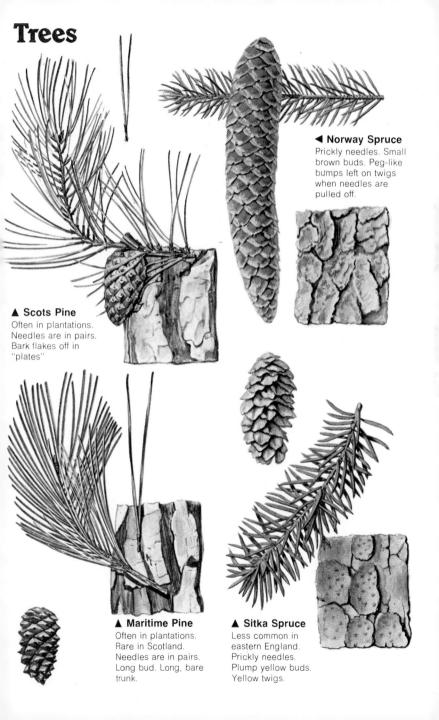

◄ Norway Spruce
Prickly needles. Small brown buds. Peg-like bumps left on twigs when needles are pulled off.

▲ Scots Pine
Often in plantations. Needles are in pairs. Bark flakes off in "plates"

▲ Maritime Pine
Often in plantations. Rare in Scotland. Needles are in pairs. Long bud. Long, bare trunk.

▲ Sitka Spruce
Less common in eastern England. Prickly needles. Plump yellow buds. Yellow twigs.

90

▼ European Larch
Deciduous. Bunches of soft, light green needles leave small knobs on twigs when they fall.

▲ Douglas Fir
Soft, fragrant needles. Cones have three-pointed bracts on each scale.

▼ European Silver Fir
Rare in east and south-east England. Needles are green above, silvery below.

▲ Corsican Pine
Often in plantations. Needles are in pairs. Onion-shaped buds.

Cone

▼ Yew
Often planted in churchyards.
Leaves and berries are poisonous.

▲ Juniper
Needles are in threes
with white band on
upper surface.
Berry-like cones.

▼ English Oak
Less common in
northern Scotland.
Acorns have long
stalks. Leaves are
short-stalked.

Acorn

▲ Chile Pine
Also called Monkey Puzzle. Stiff,
leathery leaves with sharp points.

▼ Common Ash
Less common in northern Scotland. Seeds are in clusters called "keys".

Seeds

Flowers

▼ Rowan
Clusters of flowers appear in May. Berries ripen in August.

Rowan flower

▲ Common Alder
Always found near water. Reddish catkins ripen to cone-like fruits.

Fruit →

Acorn

▲ Sessile Oak
Acorn is usually stalkless. Leaves are long-stalked.

▼ Aspen
Often grows in thickets. Leaves tremble in the wind. White downy catkins appear in May on female trees.

Catkin

▲ Goat Willow
Common on damp waste ground and in scrub woodland. Catkins, known as Pussy Willows, appear in late winter.

▼ White Willow
Common by water. Not in north-west Scotland. Weeping Willow is a variety of this species.

Catkin

Catkin

▲ Silver Birch
Catkins, known as "lamb's tails", are yellow with pollen in April. Bark peels off in ribbons.

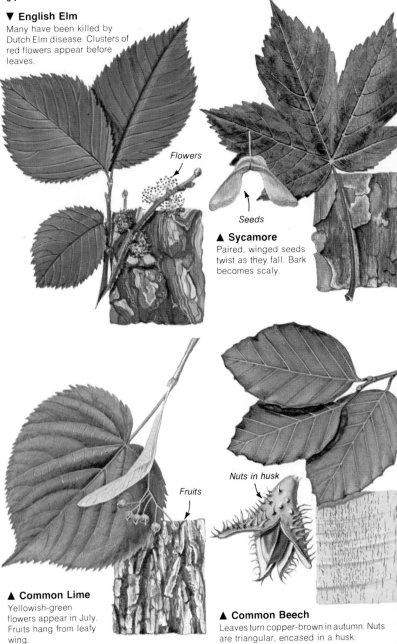

▼ English Elm
Many have been killed by Dutch Elm disease. Clusters of red flowers appear before leaves.

Flowers

▲ Sycamore
Paired, winged seeds twist as they fall. Bark becomes scaly.

Seeds

▲ Common Lime
Yellowish-green flowers appear in July. Fruits hang from leafy wing.

Fruits

Nuts in husk

▲ Common Beech
Leaves turn copper-brown in autumn. Nuts are triangular, encased in a husk.

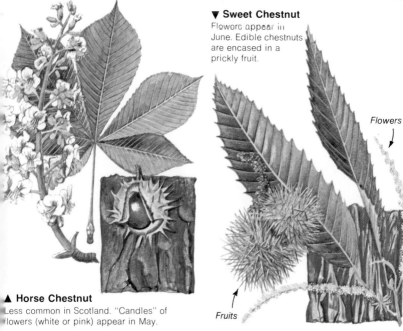

▼ Sweet Chestnut
Flowers appear in June. Edible chestnuts are encased in a prickly fruit.

Flowers

Fruits

▲ Horse Chestnut
Less common in Scotland. "Candles" of flowers (white or pink) appear in May.

▲ Holly
Less common in northern Scotland. Evergreen. Berries found only on female trees.

Flowers

▲ Common Hawthorn
Grows in thickets and hedgerows. Berries usually have only one stone.

The leaves and bark of each of the species shown below are illustrated on page 89–95.

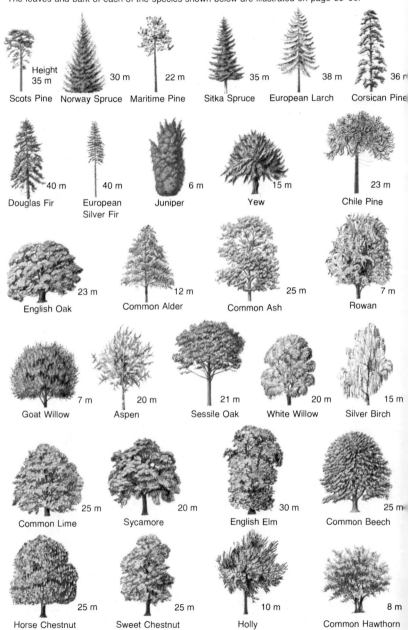

Height
35 m
Scots Pine

30 m
Norway Spruce

22 m
Maritime Pine

35 m
Sitka Spruce

38 m
European Larch

36 m
Corsican Pine

40 m
Douglas Fir

40 m
European
Silver Fir

6 m
Juniper

15 m
Yew

23 m
Chile Pine

23 m
English Oak

12 m
Common Alder

25 m
Common Ash

7 m
Rowan

7 m
Goat Willow

20 m
Aspen

21 m
Sessile Oak

20 m
White Willow

15 m
Silver Birch

25 m
Common Lime

20 m
Sycamore

30 m
English Elm

25 m
Common Beech

25 m
Horse Chestnut

25 m
Sweet Chestnut

10 m
Holly

8 m
Common Hawthorn

Places to Visit

This section describes a selection of places to observe wildlife in Wales. The sites include good examples of a wide variety of habitats and also nature reserves, country parks, birdwatching areas, museums, zoos and gardens. The majority of the sites are fairly easily accessible and many have nature trails, forest walks or visitor centres.

The descriptions of the places to visit are grouped by county in alphabetical order. Each place is marked by a number on a map which appears at the beginning of the section for each county. Notable long distance footpaths are also marked but are not numbered; their descriptions are found immediately below the maps.

The descriptions outline the main points of interest in each place and give some idea of the plants and animals that may be found there. The organizations which appear at the beginning of an entry manage, lease or own the site. All National Nature Reserves are managed by the Nature Conservancy Council but the land may be leased from another organization; this organization appears in brackets.

At the end of each entry are details about the location, approach by road and any restrictions on opening times. In most cases, the Ordnance Survey (1:50 000) map number and grid reference is given at the very end of the description (eg. OS 142; 205 800). The sheet number follows after "OS" and the grid reference after the colon. The grid references are usually for car parks or other points of access.

The visitor to nature reserves is reminded that the reserve exists to protect the habitat and its wildlife. Great care should therefore be taken on reserves, and any conditions and restrictions on access should be strictly adhered to. For some reserves, a permit may have to be obtained in advance. This is indicated where it applies, together with details of where to apply for permission. (See also the Country Code and points about nature conservation on page 122.)

Further information on the sites listed, and other places of interest in Wales, can be obtained from Tourist Information Centres, National Park Information Centres and Forestry Commission Visitor Centres. Most of the nature trails and forest walks have an accompanying leaflet or booklet. If these publications are not available on the site, an address from which they can be obtained is given, either at the end of the entry or on page 123.

The Wales Tourist Board also publishes a range of helpful literature; their address and the addresses of other useful organizations are given on page 123.

Clwyd

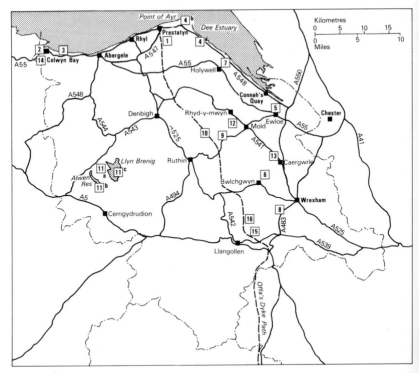

Offa's Dyke Path

Long distance footpath along the Welsh/ English border from Prestatyn to Sedbury Cliffs, near Chepstow. Named after an eighth-century earthwork. Interesting changes in geology and spectacular views. In Clwyd, the path crosses lime-stone grassland, acid moorland and forest on Silurian Shales. See also Clwyd 15 and 16 and entries in Gwent and Powys. Leaflets from: Countryside Commission and Clwyd County Council. Further infor-mation from: Offa's Dyke Association, West Street, Knighton, Powys.
☐ 173 miles/274 km. Takes 2–3 weeks to walk but many shorter walks possible. OS 116/7 126, 137, 148, 161/2.

1 Bishopswood Nature Trail

Trail exploring deciduous woodland, limestone grassland, old lead mines and quarries on Carboniferous Limestone. Part of a Site of Special Scientific Interest. Many flowers including Bloody Cranesbill, Burnet Rose, Greater Celandine and Ploughman's Spikenard. Above the tree line grow Ragwort, Rockrose and yellow Agrimony. A wide variety of woodland birds; Blackcap, Chiffchaff and Warblers are spring migrants. Many butterflies in summer. Fossils such as corals and crinoids can be seen in the limestone. Booklet from: Rhuddlan Borough Council, Tourist Information Office, Town Hall, Rhyl.
☐ Take unclassified road off A547 in centre of Prestatyn. Trail starts above St Melyd Golf Course, Meliden. OS 116: 063 813.

2 Bryn Euryn Nature Trail

North Wales Naturalists' Trust and Colwyn Borough Council. Interesting trail between Rhos-on-Sea and Mochdre, in an area which is a Site of Special Scientific Inter-est. Habitats include quarries in Carboniferous Limestone, deciduous woods and limestone grassland. A variety of woodland birds. Also many wild flowers such as Stinking Iris, Hoary Rockrose, Purging Flax and several orchids. Butterflies and moths may be seen along the trail in summer. Leaflet from: Prince of Wales Information Centre, Abergele Road, Colwyn Bay (Tel: Colwyn Bay 30478).

□ 1 mile/2 km north-west of Colwyn Bay on unclassified road off A546 or A55. OS 116: 834 798.

3 Colwyn Bay
The shore is good for watching ducks in winter and waders in autumn. Winter birds may include Purple Sandpiper, Red-throated Diver, Velvet Scoter, Common Scoter and Knot. Best viewing points between Rhos and Llanddulas.

□ Off A55. OS 116: 843 809 to 928 783.

4 Dee Estuary
Good birdwatching site for wading birds and wildfowl including Bar-tailed Godwit, Purple Sandpiper, Pintail and Wigeon. Grey Seals may sometimes be seen here. Booklet from: National Museum of Wales, Cardiff (see Mid and South Glamorgan 6).

a) Mostyn to Ffynnongroyw
Access off A548. OS 116: 162 804 and 141 821.

b) Point of Ayr
The mudflats and sands are good for watching waders, especially at high tide. Some seashells on sandy beach such as Baltic Tellin, Peppery Furrow Shell and Sword Razor. Variety of saltmarsh plants.
□ 8 miles/13 km east of Rhyl on unclassified road off A548. OS 116: 12 85.

5 Ewloe Castle Nature Trail
Trail exploring farmland, a wooded valley and a pond on acid Coal Measure Sandstones. Plants include Bluebell, Primrose and Yellow Flag. Fossils of plants such as Club Mosses, Horse-tails and Seed-ferns may be seen along the trail. Leaflet from: Clwyd County Council.
□ 9 miles/14 km west of Chester on A55, north-west of Ewloe roundabout. OS 117: 292 670.

6 Geological Museum of North Wales
Displays of a wide range of rocks and fossils from North Wales. There is also a geological trail in a quarry nearby.
□ Bwlchgwyn, near Wrexham (Tel: Wrexham 757571/3). Open daily. Sunday in winter by appointment only. 5 miles/8 km north-west of Wrexham on A525. OS 117: 259 534.

7 Holywell Nature Trail
Trail exploring a stream valley and several ponds with marshy ground and some woodland nearby. Many wild flowers including Angelica, Water Dropwort and Meadowsweet. Booklet from: Clwyd County Council.
□ Start behind Holywell High School, off A55. OS 116: 195 764.

8 Legacy Nature Trail
Trail along man-made embankments around an electricity substation. Trees include Alder, Birch, Guelder Rose and Wild Cherry. Many birds such as Barn Owl, Tawny Owl, Mistle Thrush and Yellowhammer. Leaflet from: Central Electricity Generating Board, Stockport.
□ Visits by prior arrangement with District Engineer at the above address. 3 miles/5 km south-west of Wrexham on A483 and B5426. OS 117: 293 484.

9 Loggerheads Country Park
Park in a steep gorge cut by the River Alyn with deciduous woods and conifer plantations. Also old lead-mining areas and Carboniferous Limestone quarries. Part of the park is a Site of Special Scientific Interest. Woodland flowers include Toothwort and Wood Garlic. Common Rockrose and Wild Thyme may be found on limestone outcrops. Many woodland birds in summer such as Grasshopper Warbler and Pied Flycatcher. Dipper and Kingfisher feed in the river. Nature Trail booklet from: Clwyd County Council.
□ 3 miles/5 km south-west of Mold on A494. OS 116: 198 626.

10 Moel Famau Country Park
Forestry Commission and Clwyd County Council. Large area of open moorland with

a mixed conifer woodland, a reservoir and a forest trail. Flowers include Harebell, Heath Bedstraw and Tormentil. Leaflet on forest trail from: Forestry Commission, Aberystwyth and on site.

☐ 3½ miles/5 km north-east of Ruthin. Turn north off A494. OS 116: 174 612.

11 Mynydd Hiraethog

Large area of open moorland with Forestry Commission conifer plantations,bogs,and Welsh Water Authority reservoirs.

a) Moorland area

Variety of wet moorland plants such as Bog Asphodel and Cross-leaved Heath. Good place for watching birds such as Buzzard, Raven and Red Grouse; summer visitors include Curlew and Wheatear.

☐ North of Cerrigydrudion on B4501. Access restricted to public footpaths. OS 116.

b) Alwen Reservoir

Reservoir with a Visitor Centre and walks through Forestry Commission plantations. A variety of bird life.

☐ 2 miles/3 km north of Cerrigydrudion, west off B4501. OS 116: 955 530.

c) Llyn Brenig

Large reservoir with a nature reserve at the north end. Birds include ducks, grebes and Grey Heron. Booklet on nature trail from: Llyn Brenig Centre.

☐ Permit for nature reserve from the centre. Centre open daily in afternoon. 4 miles/6.5 km north of Cerrigydrudion. Access off B4501. OS 116: 966 543.

12 Rhyd-y-mwyn Nature Trail

Trail following the River Alyn through an area of Carboniferous Limestone. Particularly good place for mosses and ferns including Beech Fern and Oak Fern. Many wild flowers such as Yellow Archangel, Crosswort and Early Purple Orchid. A wide variety of birds including Dipper, Crossbill, Nuthatch, Nightjar and Redstart (summer). Many trees including Wellingtonia. Fossil crinoids may be seen in Pandy Quarry. Booklet from: Clwyd County Council.

☐ Circular route to and from Rhyd-y-mwyn, 2 miles/3 km north-west of Mold on A541. OS 116 and 117: 206 669.

13 Waun-y-Llyn Country Park

An upland area of acid heathland and peat bog with two quarries and a small lake. Typical plants include Gorse, Bell Heather, Ling and Bilberry.

☐ Caergwrle. 6 miles/9.5 km north-west of Wrexham off A541. Turn west onto unclassified road just north of Caergwrle. OS 117: 285 580.

14 Welsh Mountain Zoo

Zoo set in a wooded estate with a wide range of animals. There is a particularly good collection of birds of prey, a reptile house and a children's zoo. A variety of local wildlife may be seen in the wooded areas. Birds include Kingfisher, Barn Owl, Raven, Sparrowhawk and Lesser Spotted Woodpecker.

☐ Colwyn Bay (Tel: Colwyn Bay 2938). Open daily. On unclassified road south off A55. OS 116: 837 778.

15 World's End to Trefor

A spectacular limestone escarpment with a deep gorge at the extreme northern end. A wide variety of typical limestone flowers such as Carline Thistle, Mullein and Purging Flax. Ferns in the gorge include some less common species such as Brittle Bladder Fern and Black and Green Spleenwort. Birds typical of open country and conifer plantations; also migrants in autumn. Mammals include Hare, Polecat and Pygmy Shrew.

☐ North of Llangollen on unclassified road off A539. Offa's Dyke Path provides access to this area. OS 117: 232 432.

16 World's End Nature Trail

The trail crosses a variety of habitats including acid moorland, cliffs and conifer plantations. Along the gorge are openings of old lead mines. Plants include Butterwort on wet ground and Bilberry and Crowberry on the moors. Birds such as Raven and Red Grouse may be seen here. Leaflet from: North Wales Naturalists' Trust.

☐ Start at the ford on unclassified road between Llangollen and Minera. Open May–September. 2½ miles/4 km north of Llangollen. OS 117: 232 478.

Dyfed

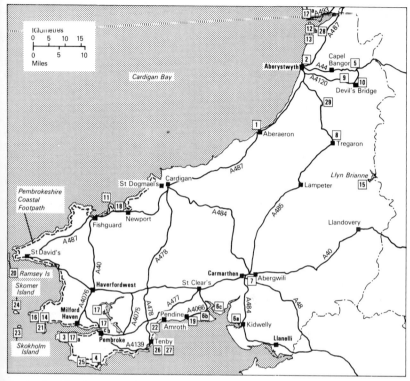

Kilometres
0 5 10 15

0 5 10
Miles

Cardigan Bay

Capel Bangor

Aberystwyth

Devil's Bridge

Aberaeron

Tregaron

Cardigan

St Dogmael's

Llyn Brianne

Pembrokeshire Coastal Footpath

Fishguard

Newport

Lampeter

Llandovery

St David's

Ramsey Is

Skomer Island

Haverfordwest

Carmarthen

St Clear's

Abergwili

Milford Haven

Pendine

Amroth

Kidwelly

Skokholm Island

Pembroke

Tenby

Llanelli

Pembrokeshire Coastal Footpath

A long distance footpath from St Dogmael's to Amroth. The path passes through a rich variety of habitats as it winds around the cliffs, bays and inlets of one of the most spectacular coasts in Britain. Good views of seabird colonies on the cliffs and the chance of seeing Grey Seals, dolphins and possibly even whales swimming offshore. Many interesting flowers, butterflies and moths may be seen along the path. See pages 20–24 and also Dyfed 16, 21 and 25. Some sections of the path are difficult and hazardous – see page 121. An excellent book, with maps, is *The Pembrokeshire Coast Path* by John. H. Barrett published for the Countryside Commission by HMSO. A wide range of publications is available from the Information Office, Pembrokeshire Coast National Park Department, County Offices, Haverfordwest (Tel: Haverfordwest 3131).
□ 168 miles/270 km. Many car parks along the route. OS 145, 157, 158.

1 Aberaeron Marine Aquarium

Marine life from Cardigan Bay including fish, shellfish and Sea Anemones.
□ The Quay, Aberaeron (Tel: Aberaeron 570608). Open daily, Easter–September.

2 Aberystwyth, Constitution Hill

Nature trail through coastal grassland and a small wood. Ferns are found in damp shady places in an old quarry and woodland flowers include Golden Saxifrage and Wood Garlic. A variety of coastal and clifftop flowers such as Dwarf Furze, English Stonecrop, Sea Campion and Valerian. Resident birds include Cormorant and Great Black-backed Gull. Examples of summer visitors are Blackcap and

Chiffchaff. Booklet from: West Wales Naturalists' Trust.

☐Trail starts from the north end of the promenade, off B4346. OS 135: 584 823.

3 Angle, West Angle Bay

A sandy bay with an interesting rocky shore on the north side. Seashells that may be found alive include Common Grey Chiton, Blue-rayed Limpet, European Cowrie and Thick Topshell (see page 22).

☐9 miles/14.5 km west of Pembroke on unclassified road off B4320. OS 157: 852 032.

4 Bosherston Lakes

National Trust. Unusual lakes on Carboniferous Limestone. The lakes are fed by underground springs so the water is very pure. A variety of aquatic plants including White Water-lily and Stonewort. An interesting range of aquatic invertebrates can be found here as well as Perch, Pike, Roach and eels.

☐4 miles/7 km south of Pembroke on unclassified road off B4319. OS 158: 968 948.

5 Bwlch Nant-yr-Arian Forest Trail

Forestry Commission trail exploring woodland, moorland and a small lake. On the migration routes of Swallow, Fieldfare and Redwing. Buzzard, Raven and the occasional Red Kite may be seen at most times of the year. Leaflet from: Forest Visitor Centre on site.

☐Visitor Centre open daily, Easter–October. Trail in Rheidol Forest, 10 miles/16 km east of Aberystwyth on A44. OS 135: 718 813.

6 Carmarthen, Estuaries of Gwendraeth, Taf and Twyi Rivers

Good sites for watching wading birds and wildfowl, particularly in winter. Birds can include Bar-tailed and Black-tailed Godwit, Golden Plover and Wigeon.

a) Gwendraeth Estuary

Access near Salmon Point Scar. 2½ miles/4 km west of Kidwelly on unclassified road off A484. OS 159: 368 070.

b) Taf Estuary

Access at Laugharne. 2 miles/3 km south of St Clear's on A4066. OS 159: 302 107.

c) Twyi Estuary

Access at Llanstephan. 7 miles/11 km south-west of Carmarthen on B4312. OS 159: 353 104.

7 Carmarthen Museum

Natural history gallery, including displays on pollution and conservation, to open in 1981/2.

☐Abergwili, Dyfed. (Tel: Carmarthen 31691). Open daily, except on Sunday. 2 miles/3 km east of Carmarthen on A40. OS 159: 437 210.

8 Cors Tregaron National Nature Reserve

Nature Conservancy Council. A good example of a raised bog with interesting plants; mammals include Polecat. See also page 31. Leaflet from: Nature Conservancy Council, Aberystwyth.

☐Access to bog itself by permit only. Apply to: Nature Conservancy Council, Aberystwyth. Open access, with good views of the reserve, from the old railway line. 8 miles/13 km north-east of Lampeter on A485 and B4343 (north of Tregaron). OS 146: 694 630 – for old railway line.

9 Cwmrheidol

Nature trail around reservoir near Rheidol Hydroelectric Power Station. The trail explores mixed woodland, an old mining area and wetlands, and passes close to a Badger sett. Day field study centre and reception centre on site. Booklet from: Central Electricity Generating Board, Stockport.

☐6½ miles/10.5 km east of Aberystwyth towards Capel Bangor, on unclassified road off A44. OS 135: 698 796.

10 Devil's Bridge

A nature trail in a deep wooded gorge with a fast-flowing river and spectacular waterfalls (see page 3). Good for ferns and mosses; also lichens on tree trunks. Look out for Pied Flycatcher in the Oakwoods in summer. Leaflet from: Hafod Arms Hotel Devil's Bridge.

☐11 miles/17.5 km east of Aberystwyth on A4120 at junction with B4574. OS 135: 742 771.

11 Dinas Island
A rocky promontory with cliff-top walks (see page 20). Especially good for sea-birds such as Guillemot and Razorbill. Also a chance of seeing Choughs. Marine mammals that may be seen offshore include dolphins, Grey Seal and Porpoise. There is a marshy area between the promontory and the mainland with birds such as Reed Bunting and Grasshopper Warbler in summer. Also marsh plants including Bogbean, Bog Pimpernel and Marsh Pennywort. Look out for Early Purple Orchid in May and June. Booklet from: West Wales Naturalists' Trust.
☐3½ miles/5.5 km east of Fishguard on unclassified road off A487. OS 157: 014 401.

12 Dovey Estuary
One of the best areas in Dyfed to see wild-fowl in autumn and winter. Unusual birds include Garganey in summer and Long-tailed Duck in winter. Other winter visitors include Pintail, Pochard and Common Scoter. Wildfowl shooting may restrict access in some areas. (See Dyfed 28)
a) North Shore (Gwynedd)
A493 follows north shore. Access at Aberdyfi. OS 135: 613 960.
b) South-west Shore
Ynyslas. 3 miles/5 km north of Borth on B4353. OS 135: 605 940.

13 Dyfi National Nature Reserve
Nature Conservancy Council. Ynyslas Nature Trail explores sand dunes and a sandy beach. At very low tide the stumps of a fossil forest may be visible on Borth Beach. Typical dune plants (see page 25) and also Bog Pimpernel, the tiny Early Forget-me-not, Spring Whitlow-grass and Wild Thyme. Many butterflies, especially in June and August. Examples include Common Blue, Small Copper, Dark Green Fritillary, Peacock and Small Tortoiseshell. Polecats and Weasels live in the dunes. Interesting seashells on the sandy beach including Alder's Necklace

Shell, Banded Wedge Shell, Common Otter Shell, Faroe Sunset Shell and Tower Shell. Dolphins and Grey Seals may be seen out at sea. Visitor Information Centre with an exhibition on local wildlife. Special facilities for field studies by schools and colleges.
☐Visitor Centre open April–September. 7½ miles/12 km north of Aberystwyth on unclassified road off B4572. OS 135: 610 942.

14 Gann Flat and Musselwick, Dale
A wide range of habitats including rocky shores, saltmarshes and a shingle ridge with specialized wild flowers. Gann Flat and the river estuary are good for bird-watching, particularly waders such as Curlew, Knot, Oystercatcher, Golden Plover, Ruff and Snipe. Badger setts may be seen along the coastal footpath at Musselwick.
☐11 miles/17.5 km south-west of Haverfordwest on B4327. OS 157: 808 067.

15 Gwenffrwd and Dinas
RSPB Reserve
The reserve includes a range of habitats – Sessile Oak woods, heather and grass moorland, upland streams and rivers and mixed deciduous woodland. A chance of seeing Red Kites, Peregrine Falcons and Merlins. Buzzards, Ravens and Pied Flycatchers are common. Polecats are occasionally seen. The Dinas is a wooded conical hill separate from the main Gwenffrwd reserve. There is a nature trail and footpaths around the base of the hill beside the River Towy. Leaflet from: RSPB, Newtown, Powys.
☐The Warden, Troedrhiwgelynen, Rhandir-mwyn, Llandovery. *Gwenffrwd reserve* – Open Monday, Wednesday and Saturday, April–August. Visitors should report outside warden's house on Pumsaint Road between 10.00 and 14.00 on visiting days. 7½ miles/12 km north of Llandovery on unclassified road off A40 via Cil-y-cwm. OS 146: 749 460.
Dinas – Nature trail open spring and summer only; footpaths open daily all year. 2½ miles/4 km north of Rhandir-mwyn on unclassified road towards Llyn Brianne. OS 146: 788 470.

16 Marloes Sands Nature Trail

The trail explores sea cliffs and rocky shore habitats (see title page). Choughs and Ravens may be seen as well as Grey Seals offshore. Many butterflies including Painted Lady, Small Copper and Small Tortoiseshell. Look for Badger setts on the cliff slopes. Also a wetland area – Marloes Mere – with Fleabane and Watermint; birds include Reed Bunting and Snipe (in winter). The trail follows part of the Pembrokeshire Coastal Footpath (see pages 20–24). Leaflet from: West Wales Naturalists' Trust.
☐ 10 miles/16 km south-west of Haverfordwest on unclassified road off B4327. OS 157: 794 084.

17 Milford Haven

Several good birdwatching sites (from August–March) along the inlet and the estuaries of the Cleddau, Cresswell and Carew Rivers. Birds include Dunlin, Black-tailed Godwit, Goldeneye, Great Crested Grebe, Red-breasted Merganser, Whimbrel and Wigeon.

a) Angle
12 miles/19 km west of Pembroke on unclassified road off B4320. Angle Bay OS 157: 897 022. Angle Point OS 157: 875 033.

b) Cosheston
1½ miles/2.5 km north-east of Pembroke on unclassified road off A4075. OS 157: 003 034.

c) Cosheston Point
1 mile/1.5 km west of Cosheston on unclassified road. OS 157: 985 039.

d) Western Cleddau
Section of river between Hook, OS 157: 978 115, and Little Milford OS 157: 967 119.

18 Newport Sands

A sandy beach backed by dunes. Many empty seashells can be found on the strandline including some very small species in the shell-sand. Examples include European Cowrie, Common Slit Limpet and Small Needle Whelk. Also seashells typical of the upper part of a rocky shore on cliffs and boulders.
☐ 9 miles/14.5 km south-west of Cardigan on A487 and B4582. OS 145: 054 405.

19 Pendine Sands

A long sandy beach with sand dunes and tall limestone cliffs. Typical shells of sandy beaches (see pages 22 and 24) and also Acteon Shell, Basket Shell, Lobe Shell, Tusk Shell and White Furrow Shell. Wading birds and gulls feed on the shore.
☐ The eastern part of the beach is sometimes closed for use as a firing range. Access from Pendine at end of A4066. OS 158: 234 078.

20 Ramsey Island

A grassy island with rocky shores. Many seabirds and predatory birds (see page 22). Breeding grounds of Grey Seal on the beaches from September onwards.
☐ Access from lifeboat station at St Justinian. 2 miles/3 km west of St David's on unclassified road off A487. OS 157: 723 252.

21 St Ann's Head, Dale

A rocky promontory with cliffs, reached by part of the Pembrokeshire Coastal Footpath. Good views of seabirds including Fulmar, which breeds here, and Gannet and Manx Shearwater offshore. Many flowers including Rock Sea-lavender.
☐ 12 miles/19 km south-west of Haverfordwest on unclassified road south of B4327. OS 157: 805 028.

22 Saundersfoot Beach

A sandy beach good for seashells (see Dyfed 13). Steep tree-capped cliffs to the south of the harbour where faulting and folding of the Coal Measure Sandstones can be seen (see page 9).
☐ 2 miles/3 km north of Tenby on A478 and B4316. OS 158: 135 045.

23 Skokholm Island

West Wales Naturalists' Trust reserve. This island is noted for its fine colonies of seabirds including Puffin, Razorbill, Manx Shearwater and Storm Petrel. Other breeding species include Oystercatcher, Raven and Wheatear. An excellent point for viewing bird migration in April and May and late August to October. Many rare bird species have been recorded here. A variety of wild flowers (see page 20) and many utterflies (see next entry). Leaflet from: West Wales Naturalists' Trust.

Small hostel on the island run by West Wales Naturalists' Trust. Day visits on Monday in June and July only – details from Pembrokeshire Coast National Park Information Centre, Kingsmoor Common, Kilgetty. (Tel: Saundersfoot 812175)

24 Skomer National Nature Reserve

Nature Conservancy Council and West Wales Naturalists' Trust. The island is well known for its colonies of seabirds – see page 22. Many wild flowers on the cliffs – see page 20. Over 20 species of butterflies may be seen here including Common Blue, Dark Green Fritillary, Small Copper and Small Tortoiseshell. Other butterflies such as Clouded Yellow, Painted Lady and Red Admiral visit the island on migration flights. Grey Seals are often seen here in summer and breed here in autumn. There is a marine nature reserve around Skomer. Booklet (with information on nature trail) from: West Wales Naturalists' Trust.

Reached by boat from Martin's Haven – day trips (except Monday), weather permitting. 15 miles/24 km south-west of Haverfordwest on unclassified road off B4327. OS 157: 760 092.

25 Stack Rocks (Elegug Stacks), Castlemartin

Part of the Pembrokeshire Coastal Footpath passes close to Stack Rocks. Large colonies of seabirds, including Fulmar, Guillemot, Kittiwake and Razorbill may be seen here. Cliff-top grassland with many coastal flowers (see page 20).

3 miles/5 km south-east of Castlemartin on unclassified road off B4319. Road open Saturday, Sunday, Bank Holidays and most evenings. OS 158: 926 946.

26 Tenby Museum

An interesting collection of local cave animal remains including bones of Mammoths. Also exhibits on local birds, butterflies, seashells and geology.

Castle Hill, Tenby. (Tel: Tenby 2809). Open daily all year but, from October to March, closed Sundays.

27 Tenby, South Sands

A fine sandy beach. Many seashells; also sand dunes with some scrub areas of Sea Buckthorn. Steep limestone cliffs and caves by Castle Hill and St Catherine's Island.

Access to caves at low tide (see page 121). OS 158: 135 002.

28 Ynys-hir
RSPB Reserve

An interesting reserve with a variety of habitats and many birds including large numbers of waders and ducks on the estuary from July to April. Breeding birds include Buzzard, Sparrowhawk and Pied Flycatcher and, in winter, Hen Harrier, Merlin and Peregrine Falcon are regularly seen. A small flock of Greenland White-fronted Geese over-winter in the vicinity of the reserve. Leaflet from: RSPB, Newtown, Powys.

The Warden, Cae'r Berllan, Eglwys-fach, Glandyfi, Machynlleth, Powys. Open Wednesday, Thursday and weekends April–September; Sunday and Wednesday October–March. 7 miles/11 km south-west of Machynlleth. Turn off A487 in Furnace village. Please report to reception in Cae'r Berllan Wood on arrival. Walks start from reception point. OS 135: 683 965.

29 Ystwyth Forest, Forest Walk and Butterfly Reserve

Forestry Commission and West Wales Naturalists' Trust. The Black Covert forest walk passes by a wide range of deciduous and coniferous trees. Many woodland birds and, in open country, Buzzard and Raven may be seen. Coed Allt Fedw near the Iron Age hill fort is managed as a butterfly reserve and a suitable range of food plants for the caterpillars is encouraged. Butterflies include Common Blue, Orange Tip, Red Admiral, Small Copper, Small Pearl-bordered Fritillary, Small Skipper, and many others. Leaflet from: Forestry Commission, Aberystwyth and on site.

7 miles/11 km south-east of Aberystwyth on A487 and B4340. Cross bridge over River Ystwyth, trail starts on west side of river. OS 135: 668 728.

Mid and South Glamorgan

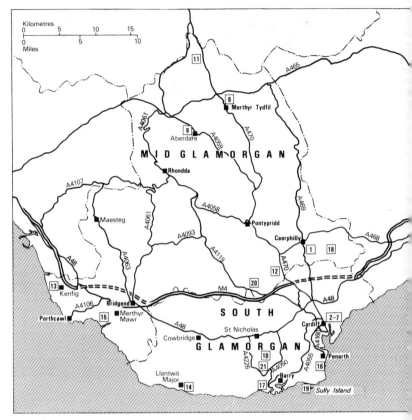

1 Caerphilly Common Nature Trail

The trail crosses a variety of rock types with different plant communities. The flowers on the Coal Measures are typical of acid moorland (see page 15). In the wet clay valley, Cross-leaved Heath, Lady's Smock and Marsh Pennywort may be found. Traveller's Joy grows on the limestone outcrops. Booklet from: Cardiff City Council.

☐ Just south of Caerphilly on the A469. OS 171: 156 853.

2 Cardiff, Bute Park

A fine park alongside the River Taff with a nature trail from Cardiff Castle to Blackweir. Many exotic trees such as Blue Gum, Maidenhair Tree and Tulip Tree. A wide variety of birds including Kestrel, Tawny Owl, Treecreeper and Siskin (on migration). The area by the castle moat is rich in wild flowers and freshwater snails. Booklet from: Cardiff City Council.

☐ Castle Street, alongside Cardiff Castle. OS 171: 182 767.

3 Cardiff Dockland

The derelict dockland provides a habitat for a surprising variety of wild flowers; many rare plants may also be seen here. A good place for watching wading birds and wildfowl on the mudflats nearby especially in winter.

☐ ½ mile/1 km south of Butetown and Grangetown off A4119. OS 171: 187 744.

4 Cardiff, Glamorgan Canal and Long Wood

A nature reserve with a nature trail. The banks of the disused canal are rich in wild-life. Flowers include Arrowhead and Yellow Water-lily in the canal, with Police-man's Helmet and Purple Loosestrife on the banks. The canal provides a good habitat for frogs, newts, freshwater sponges, sticklebacks, water snails and Water Voles. Kingfishers also feed in the canal. Long Wood is mainly deciduous with trees such as Ash and Beech; Alder grows by the canal. Typical woodland flowers (see page 28) and also the parasitic Toothwort. A wide variety of birds may be seen including Buzzard, Grasshopper Warbler (summer), Goldcrest, Great Spotted Woodpecker, Kestrel, Siskin (on migration) and Sparrowhawk. Booklet from: Cardiff City Council.
□ Turn west off A4054 onto unclassified road at Whitchurch. OS 171: 144 804.

5 Cardiff, Nant Fawr Walk

The walk explores parkland, gardens and Roath Park lake. Unusual trees include Maidenhair Tree and Tree of Heaven. Native and exotic wildfowl live on the lake and Kingfishers may be seen at the north-ern end. Booklet from: Cardiff City Council.
□ North-east part of Cardiff, approached by Lake Road East and Lake Road West.

6 Cardiff, National Museum of Wales

Interesting displays on Welsh geology and natural history. The museum organizes family expeditions throughout the summer in all parts of Wales.
□ Cathays Park, Cardiff (Tel: Cardiff 397951). Open daily, closed on Sunday morning.

7 Cardiff, Wenallt

An area of deciduous woodland with two nature trails. Many wild flowers including Bluebell, Foxglove, Red Campion and Vio-let. A wide variety of woodland birds such as Nuthatch, Treecreeper and several tits. Booklet from: Cardiff City Council.
□ 4 miles/6.5 km north of Cardiff city centre on unclassified road off A469. OS 171: 153 833.

8 Cyfarthfa Castle Museum

Small natural history section with birds, small mammals and fish. Also cases of fossils from the South Wales Coalfield.
□ Merthyr Tydfil (Tel: Merthyr Tydfil 3112). Open daily. 1 mile/1.5 km north-west of town centre.

9 Dare Valley Country Park

Open moorland with a wooded valley on reclaimed land once used for coal mining. Ring Ouzel may be seen at Tarren-y-Bwllfa. Leaflet from: Cynon Valley District Council, Town Hall, Aberdare.
□ 1½ miles/2.5 km west of Aberdare off A4059, on unclassified road via Cwmdare. OS 170: 982 028.

10 Dyffryn Gardens

An interesting range of plants. The shrub borders and arboretum contain species rarely seen growing outdoors in Britain. The plant houses contain a variety of trop-ical, temperate and cool house plants including many orchids and cacti.
□ St Nicholas, near Cardiff (Tel: Cardiff 593328). Open daily mid-May–August. Afternoons only in April, early May and September. Weekends only in October. 5 miles/8km west of Cardiff on unclassi-fied road south off A48. OS 171: 096 728.

11 Garwnant Forest Centre and Walks

Forestry Commission. Interesting centre with exhibitions and slide shows. Also for-est walks through deciduous woods, con-ifer plantations and along the Llwyn-on Reservoir. Publications available on site.
□ Garwnant, Cwm Taf, Merthyr Tydfil (Tel: Merthyr Tydfil 3060). Open daily Easter–September, afternoons only at weekends. 6 miles/9 km north of Merthyr Tydfil on unclassified road west off A470. OS 160: 003 131.

12 Garth Hill

Grassy moorland. A good site for watching birds typical of open country such as Buz-zard, Kestrel, Lapwing and Meadow Pipit.
□ 7 miles/11 km north of Cardiff city centre on unclassified road to Pentyrch. Turn west off A470 north-west of Tongwynlais. OS 171: 108 834.

13 Kenfig Pool and Dunes
Nature Reserve and Site of Special Scientific Interest. Interesting habitat for birds and flowers, especially orchids. Also Sharp Sea Rush, ferns and fungi such as Puffballs and Morel. For more details on the wildlife see page 29. Publications available at the Reserve Centre on site. Further information from the Warden (Tel: Kenfig Hill 743386 or Cardiff 28033).
□7½ miles/12 km west of Bridgend on unclassified roads off A48. OS 170: 803 813.

14 Llantwit Major
Some interesting marine life in rock pools on Col-huw beach. Cliffs of Liassic Limestone (see page 9) with plants such as Rock Samphire, Rock Sea - lavender and Thrift. A good site for butterflies in summer. A range of ferns and wall plants on limestone walls in the village. Leaflet from: Kenfig Reserve Centre (see previous entry).
□9 miles/14 km west of Barry on B4265. OS 170: 957 674.

15 Merthyr Mawr
Extensive sand dune system with some scrub areas of Sea Buckthorn. Brown-lipped Snails are common; their shells may be found on Thrush anvils. Many dune slack areas with Creeping Willow.
□3 miles/5 km south-west of Bridgend on B4524. OS 170: 872 774.

16 Penarth to Lavernock Point
At low tide it is possible to walk along the beach to examine the geology of the Triassic marls and look for fossil ammonites and bivalves in the beach pebbles. The cliff path is good for butterflies in summer.
□4 miles/6 km south of Cardiff on A4160. OS 171: 187 706.

17 Porthkerry Country Park
A valley near the sea with meadows and deciduous woodland. A wide variety of plants including a few rare species. Cliff Wood is a Site of Special Scientific Interest containing Ash, Oak and Yew. Also some interesting Liassic Limestone cliffs, which are rich in fossils; ammonites and bivalves

may be found on the beach below. Many birds including Buzzard and Raven may be seen here. Booklet from: the Warden, Nightingale Cottage, Porthkerry Country Park, Barry (Tel: Barry 733589).
□Just west of Barry on unclassified road off A4055. OS 170: 086 668.

18 Rudry
Walks through two Forestry Commission plantations, Coed Coesau-whips and Craig-y-Llan. The broad woodland rides and areas of young trees are good for butterflies such as Large Skipper, Green-veined White and Silver-washed Fritillary. Many woodland birds. Leaflet from: Forestry Commission, Cardiff.
□3 miles/5 km east of Caerphilly on unclassified road off A468. OS 171 202 854.

19 Sully Island and Causeway
The island is reached at low tide by the causeway; take care with the incoming tide (see page 121). Wildlife on the rocky shore includes Barnacles, Crabs, Tube Worms, typical shells (see page 22) and brown seaweeds. Many coastal birds and also Goldfinch, Greenfinch and Linnet or the grassland and bushes of the island.
□3 miles/5 km east of Barry or unclassified road off B4267. OS 171 167 674.

20 Ty'n-y-Coed Forest Walk
Forestry Commission and Pentyrch Civic Trust. Walk through deciduous and coniferous woodland with many flowers such as Bluebell, Traveller's Joy, Lesser Celandine and Wood Anemone. A wide variety of woodland birds. Mammals include Badger and Grey Squirrel. Leaflet from: Forestry Commission, Cardiff.
□8½ miles/14 km north-west of Cardiff off A4119 on unclassified road via Creigiau. OS 170: 083 826.

21 Welsh Hawking Centre
Good collection of birds of prey and wild fowl. Also big cats and chimpanzees.
□Weycock Road, Barry (Tel: Barry 734687). Open daily. 2 miles/3 km north west of Barry on A4226. OS 171: 094 693

West Glamorgan

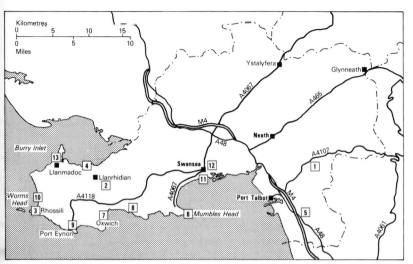

1 Afan Argoed Park
Forestry Commission and West Glamorgan County Council. Several walks through woodland in Afan Valley, a former coal mining area. A variety of birds; mammals include Fallow Deer. Many fungi can be found in the woods in autumn. Flowers include Ivy-leaved Bellflower and Monkey Flower. Booklet from: Countryside Centre on site.

□ Cynonville, Port Talbot (Tel: Cymmer 850564). Countryside Centre open daily, Easter–October, weekends only in winter. 5 miles/8 km north-east of Port Talbot on A4107. OS 170: 814 949.

2 Cillibion, Broad Pool
Glamorgan Naturalists' Trust nature reserve. A small pool with Fringed Water-lily, Water Spider, Damselflies and over 20 species of Dragonflies. Moorland around the pool; plants include Marsh Pennywort, Marsh Violet and Bog Myrtle.

□ 10 miles/16 km west of Swansea on unclassified road south of B4271. OS 159: 510 910.

3 Gower Coast National Nature Reserve
Nature Conservancy Council (National Trust). See also West Glamorgan 10.
a) Limestone Nature Trail

Circular walk from Rhossili. Many flowers on the cliffs including Hoary Rockrose and Yellow Whitlow-grass. Look for fossils in the limestone walls. Leaflet from: Oxwich Reserve Centre, Oxwich, Gower, Swansea. (Tel: Gower 320).
b) Worms Head
Accessible at low tide (see page 121). Rocky shore on the causeway (see page 22). Gulls and wading birds come here to feed. Plants on the island include Bluebell and Rock Sea Spurrey. Guillemots and Razorbills nest on the cliffs.

□ Rhossili is 20 miles/32 km west of Swansea on B4247. OS 159: 414 881.

4 Llanrhidian Marsh and Burry Inlet
Nature Conservancy Council (National Trust). The saltmarsh and mudflats provide a good site for waders and wildfowl. Birds include Brent Geese, Eider Duck, Goldeneye, Pintail, Teal, Godwits and Whimbrel. Many coastal plants (see pages 27 and 28). Cockle fishers with their carts may be seen here.

□ 10 miles/16 km west of Swansea. Access on unclassified roads off B4295. OS 159: 514 944.

5 Margam Park
A large area of mixed woodland and grass-

land with streams and lakes. Birds include Buzzard, Kestrel and the occasional Sparrowhawk; ducks and swans may be seen on the lakes and there is a Heronry in the conifers beside Furzemill Pond. Mammals include Badger, Hare and a large herd of Fallow Deer. Adders may also be seen in the park. Booklets are available on the site.
☐ Margam, Port Talbot (Tel: Port Talbot 71635). Open daily, except Monday, April-September; also closed Tuesday in winter. 2 miles/3 km south-east of Port Talbot. Turn east off A48. OS 170: 801 863.

6 Mumbles Head
Carboniferous Limestone cliffs near the pier with flowers such as Musk Thistle, Portland Spurge, Perforate St John's Wort and the rare Sea Stock. A good place to view migrant birds such as Purple Sandpiper and Terns. Causeway to the Middle and Outer Heads at the pier (see page 121). Rocky shores on the island (see page 22).
☐ 3 miles/5 km south-west of Swansea on A4067 and B4433. OS 159: 631 874.

7 Oxwich National Nature Reserve
Nature Conservancy Council. A range of contrasting habitats: saltmarsh, freshwater marsh, pools, deciduous woodland, sea cliffs, sand dunes and sandy and rocky shores (see pages 25-28). Many seashells can be found on the beach. Two nature trails explore the area. Leaflets from: Oxwich Reserve Centre, Oxwich, Swansea (Tel: Gower 320).
☐ Marshes and pools accessible to permit holders only. Apply to: Nature Conservancy Council, Cardiff. 10 miles/16 km south-west of Swansea on unclassified road south off A4118. OS 159: 503 864.

8 Parkmill to Three Cliffs Bay
An unusual walk following the river down the Pennard Valley, a Site of Special Scientific Interest. Deciduous woods, sand dunes (Pennard Burrows) and a small saltmarsh near the beach (see page 25). Rich plant life on Carboniferous Limestone.
☐ 7½ miles/12 km south-west of Swansea on A4118. OS 159: 543 892.

9 Port Eynon
National Trust and Glamorgan Naturalists' Trust. Cliffs of Carboniferous Limestone with a rich variety of coastal flowers including Hoary Rockrose and Yellow Whitlow-grass (see also page 25). Also many butterflies in spring and summer. Seaweeds and marine animals can be found on the rocky shore (see page 22).
☐ 15 miles/24 km south-west of Swansea on A4118. OS 159: 468 852.

10 Rhossili Bay
A sandy beach rich in seashells, particularly the Banded Wedge Shell. Also Necklace Shells, European Cowries, Striped Venus and Trough Shells. (See also West Glamorgan 3.)
☐ 20 miles/32 km west of Swansea on A4118 and B4247. OS 159: 414 881.

11 Swansea Bay
An area of sand and mudflats at low tide, particularly good for seashells such as Acteon Shell, Arctic Cyprina, Baltic Tellin, Peppery Furrow Shell, Pullet Carpet Shell and Striped Venus.
☐ Coastline between The Mumbles and Swansea off A4067. OS 159.

12 Swansea Museum
Natural history collection includes birds and seashells.
☐ Victoria Road, Swansea (Tel: Swansea 53763). Open daily, except Sunday.

13 Whiteford National Nature Reserve
Nature Conservancy Council. An extensive sand dune system with forestry plantations, a sandy shore and some saltmarsh. Typical dune plants (see pages 25 and 27) and also Early Marsh Orchid, Fen Orchid and Marsh Helleborine. Many spiders and rich insect life including Glow-worms, Cinnabar Moths and a variety of butterflies. Leaflet available on the site.
☐ Permit needed for parts of the reserve away from footpaths. Apply to: Nature Conservancy Council, Cardiff. 15 miles/24 km west of Swansea on unclassified road off B4271. Parking in Llanmadoc village. OS 159: 443 933.

Gwent

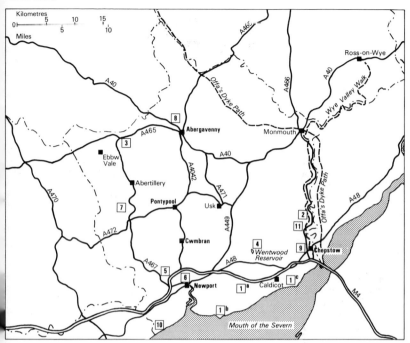

Kilometres 0 5 10 15
Miles 5 10

Ross-on-Wye
Offa's Dyke Path
A465
A466
A40
Wye Valley Walk
A40
8 Abergavenny
Monmouth
A465 3
Ebbw Vale
A40
Abertillery
A4042
A471
7 Pontypool
Usk
Offa's Dyke Path
A48
A470
A472
A449
2
11
Cwmbran
4 Wentwood Reservoir
9 Chepstow
A467
A48
5
6 1ᵃ Caldicot 1ᶜ
Newport
1ᵇ
10
Mouth of the Severn
M4

Offa's Dyke Path

North of Monmouth, the path crosses the Black Mountains – an area of upland grassland (see page 15). For details, see entry at beginning of Clwyd.

Wye Valley Walk

An interesting long distance footpath from Chepstow to Monmouth. (The path continues to Ross-on-Wye.) See also Gwent 2 and 11. Route cards from: Gwent County Council, County Hall Cwmbran.
□ 34 miles/55 km. OS 162.

1 Caldicot Levels

An ancient series of freshwater ditches or reens, which drain the fields on low ground behind the sea wall. Rich in aquatic plants and animals including water snails, insect larvae and eels.

a) Magor

South of the village, the vegetation includes Frogbit, Water Fern, Reedmace and Yellow Flag. The area is also good for birdwatching: Goldfinch, Grey Heron, Reed Bunting and many others.
□ 4½ miles/7 km east of Newport on unclassified roads off B4245. OS 171: 41 86.

b) Goldcliff

A good site for watching wading birds and wildfowl including Curlew, Dunlin, Knot, Pochard, Redshank and Shelduck.
□ 3 miles/5 km south-east of Newport on unclassified road off A455. OS 171: 362 827.

c) Sudbrook Fort

Good birdwatching area. See Goldcliff (previous entry).
□ Near Portskewett, 4 miles/6 km south-west of Chepstow on unclassified road off A48. OS 172: 505 873.

2 Chapel Hill

A Forestry Commission walk in Tintern Forest. Mixed woodland with a variety of birds; flowers include Coltsfoot, Golden Saxifrage and Wood Spurge. Particularly good for mosses and ferns. Leaflet from: Forestry Commission, Cardiff.

☐5 miles/8 km north of Chepstow. Turn west off A466 at Tintern onto unclassified road. OS 162: 527 002.

3 Cwm Clydach National Nature Reserve

Nature Conservancy Council. A long gorge through Carboniferous Limestone. Mainly Beech woodland with some Sessile Oak, Yew and species of Whitebeam found only in the Brecon region. Leaflet from: Nature Conservancy Council, Cardiff.
☐Permit needed to visit parts of the reserve away from footpaths. Apply to: Nature Conservancy Council, Cardiff. 7 miles/11km west of Abergavenny on A465. OS 161: 205 123.

4 Gray Hill Countryside Trail

Trail in Wentwood Forest through coniferous plantations and across the open heathland on Gray Hill. A wide variety of woodland birds and, on the heath, birds such as Buzzard, Kestrel and Raven. Woodland mammals include Badger and Grey Squirrel. Leaflet from: Gwent County Council, County Hall, Cwmbran.
☐8 miles/13 km north-east of Newport, on unclassified road north off A48. Trail starts at Wentwood Reservoir. OS 171: 430 938.

5 Newport, Monmouthshire and Brecon Canal

Interesting freshwater habitat for aquatic life and waterside plants (see pages 16 and 18).
☐Off A467 on north-western outskirts of Newport. OS 171: 279 886.

6 Newport Museum

Natural history collection includes good displays on the woodland life and bird life of Gwent. Also interesting exhibits on local geology.
☐John Frost Square, Newport (Tel: Newport 840064). Open daily, except Sunday.

7 Pen-y-Fan Country Park

Dry heathland and marshy areas rich in wildlife, particularly near the pond and stream. Birds include Warblers in summer and Whooper Swan in winter. Leaflet from:

Gwent County Council, County Hall, Cwmbran.
☐7 miles/11 km west of Pontypool on A472. Turn off B4251 onto unclassified road. OS 171: 195 004.

8 St Mary's Vale Nature Trail

National Trust. The trail explores a steep-sided wooded valley and open moorland on Sugar Loaf in the Black Mountains. Sessile Oak in the wood and typical moorland plants (see page 15). Birds include Buzzard, Chiffchaff and Skylark. Leaflet from: Brecon Beacons National Park Authority, Brecon.
☐1½ miles/2.5 km north-west of Abergavenny on unclassified road north off A40. Please use car park past Llwyn-du Reservoir. OS 161: 284 162.

9 St Pierre's Great Wood

Forestry Commission. An interesting walk through mixed woodland. Clearings in the wood are good places to see butterflies in summer.
☐2 miles/3 km south-west of Chepstow on unclassified road north off A48. OS 162: 505 930.

10 Wentloog Levels

An extensive series of reens on the coastal plain between Cardiff and Newport, which is rich in aquatic life. Some saltmarsh vegetation and tidal mudflats where wading birds and wildfowl feed.
☐East of Cardiff, take B4239 to Peterstone Wentloog. OS 171: 268 803.

11 Wyndcliff Nature Trail

Forestry Commission, Gwent Trust for Nature Conservation and Nature Conservancy Council. Trail along a river cliff of Carboniferous Limestone. Deciduous woodland with flowers including Traveller's Joy, Sweet Woodruff and Wood Melick (see also page 28). A wide variety of birds such as Pied Flycatcher and Goldcrest. This is also a good place for butterflies including Common Blue, Holly Blue and Silver-washed Fritillary. Leaflet from: Nature Conservancy Council, Cardiff.
☐3 miles/5 km north of Chepstow on A466. OS 162: 526 972.

Gwynedd

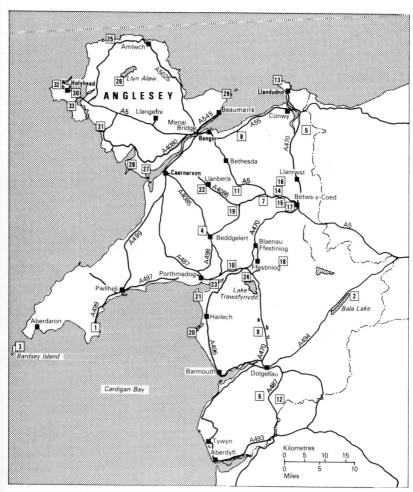

1 Abersoch Beach

A stretch of sandy beach backed by sand dunes. A good site for collecting shells including Arctic Cyprina, Dog Cockle, Striped Venus Shell, Thin Tellin, Tower Shell, several Razor Shells and various species of Scallops.

☐5 miles/8 km south-west of Pwllheli on A499. OS 123: 313 282.

2 Bala Lake (Llyn Tegid)

The largest natural lake in Wales with a variety of fish such as Brown Trout, Perch and Pike. Also known for the Gwyniad (see page 32). Cormorant, Goldeneye and Grey Heron may be seen in winter and birds such as Meadow Pipit, Sedge Warbler and Whinchat nest in the surrounding hills in summer. Aquatic plants include Awlwort, Quillwort, Shoreweed, various sedges and Water Lobelia.

☐15 miles/24 km north-east of Dolgellau on A494. Parking on north side of lake. OS 125: 910 343.

3 Bardsey Bird and Field Observatory

A stay at the observatory on Bardsey Island provides many opportunities for watching breeding colonies of seabirds including Fulmar, Kittiwake and Manx Shearwater. The most interesting time to visit is in spring and autumn to see migrating birds such as Flycatchers, Goldcrest, Redwing and Warblers. Most years there are some unusual birds from America and Asia. This is also a well-known site for observing night migration. Information from: the Booking Secretary, 21a Gestridge Road, Kingsteignton, Newton Abbot (Tel: Newton Abbot 68580).

☐2 miles/3 km off south-west corner of Lleyn Peninsula. Reached by boat from Pwllheli. OS 123.

4 Beddgelert Forest

Forestry Commission plantation with forest trail and several walks. A variety of native and introduced conifers and deciduous trees such as Birch and Oak. Pine Martens live in the forest and Dipper and Wagtails may be seen on the rocks by the stream. Butterflies include Red Admiral and Small Tortoiseshell. Leaflet from: Forestry Commission, Aberystwyth.

☐Forest trail 1 mile/1.5 km north-west of Beddgelert on A4085. OS 115: 578 491. Other access points are Nant Gwynant OS 115: 635 512 and Dolfriog OS 115: 616 457.

5 Bodnant Garden

National Trust. A magnificent collection of Azaleas, Camellias, Magnolias, Rhododendrons and conifers. Also an interesting rock garden, Rose garden and unusual plants such as Gentians.

☐Bodnant (Tel: Tyn-y-Groes 460). Open daily, mid-March–October. 8 miles/13 km south of Colwyn Bay off A470. OS 116: 801 723.

6 Cader Idris National Nature Reserve

The Nature Conservancy Council manage this well known geological and botanical site. An interesting contrast between plants on acid volcanic rocks (e.g. Bilberry) and those on the more alkaline lava (e.g. Purple Saxifrage). Arctic-alpine plants such as Globeflower, Lesser Meadow-rue and Mountain Sorrel grow on cliff ledges (see also pages 10 and 11). Birds that may be seen in summer include Pied Flycatcher, Redstart, Ring Ouzel and Wheatear. Leaflet from: Nature Conservancy Council, Bangor.

☐Permit needed for enclosed woodland on the reserve. Apply to: Nature Conservancy Council, Bangor. 7 miles/11 km south of Dolgellau on A487 and B4405. OS 124: 730 114.

7 Capel Curig

A footpath from the road leads through Sessile Oak woods onto open craggy moorland. A good place to see woodland and moorland birds (see pages 11 and 12 for examples).

☐Path starts opposite Cobdens Hotel. 5 miles/8 km north-west of Betws-y-Coed on A5. OS 115: 733 573.

8 Coedydd Aber
National Nature Reserve

Nature Conservancy Council. The reserve includes Oakwoods, streams, moorland, the gorge of the Afon Rhaeadr Fawr and the Aber Falls. Many woodland birds (see page 12) and Chiffchaff and Warblers in summer. Ravens nest near the waterfall and moorland birds include Merlin and Ring Ouzel. Welsh Ponies roam in the valley. Plants include Wall Pennywort, which may be found in the rock crevices of the gorge. Leaflet from: Nature Conservancy Council, Bangor.

☐6 miles/9.5 km north-east of Bangor on unclassified road off A55. OS 115: 663 720.

9 Coed-y-Brenin Forest

Forestry Commission woodland with a Visitor Centre and several trails. Mainly conifer plantations with patches of broad-leaved trees; also open moorland, pasture and rivers. Some areas of copper-rich soil with an unexpected range of plants (see page 11). Many woodland birds (see page 12) and Black Grouse on high ground. Buzzard, Kestrel and Raven may also be seen over open ground. Mammals include Badger, Fallow Deer and Polecat – look for tracks and signs. Brown Trout live in the rivers while Dipper and Wagtails may be seen on the boulders and banks. Leaflets from: Forestry Commission, Aberystwyth or the Visitor Centre.

a) Maesgwm Visitor Centre
Exhibition on forestry practice and wildlife in the forest. Many Forestry Commission publications available.

☐Ganllwyd, Dolgellau. (Tel: Ganllwyd 210). Open Easter-September. 8 miles/ 13 km north of Dolgellau on unclassified road off A470. OS 124: 715 276.

b) Dolgefeiliau Forest Trails
Trails through mixed woodland. A variety of ferns and mosses under deciduous trees.

☐7 miles/11 km north of Dolgellau on A470. OS 124: 721 269.

c) Ty'n-y-Groes Forest Trail
A trail exploring a conifer plantation and an old deciduous wood of Beech and Sweet Chestnut. The area has a copper-rich soil, so look for stunted trees. Many mosses and liverworts on damp ground near springs; ferns include Broad Buckler, Hard Fern and Lady Fern. Nests of Wood Ants may be seen along the path.

☐5 miles/8 km north of Dolgellau on A470. OS 124: 730 233.

10 Coedydd Maentwrog National Nature Reserve

Nature Conservancy Council (National Trust). One of the few large native Oak-woods in Wales; many lichens, mosses and also ferns such as Common Polypody, which often grows on trees. Flowers in the meadow area in spring include Celandines, Primroses and Violets and butter-flies such as Fritillaries and Hairstreaks may be seen here. Leaflet from: Nature Conservancy Council, Bangor.

☐6 miles/9.5 km east of Porthmadog on A487 and B4410. OS 124: 652 416.

11 Cwm Idwal National Nature Reserve

Nature Conservancy Council. Magnificent cwm with moraines and other evidence of glacial activity. A dark cleft in the cliffs marks the base of a huge rock fold known as the Snowdon syncline. A shallow lake, Llyn Idwal, occupies the floor of the cwm.

Lakeside birds include Cormorant and gulls with Goldeneye, Pochard and other birds in winter. The reserve is famous for arctic-alpine plants (see pages 10 and 11). Feral goats graze on the reserve. Leaflet from: Nature Conservancy Council, Bangor.

☐4 miles/6.5 km south-east of Bethesda on A5. OS 115: 647 604.

12 Foel Friog Forest Trail

Forestry Commission. Walk through Dyfi Forest exploring a range of habitats including river, conifer plantation, Oak-wood and the ruins of Blue Slate quarries. Brown Trout and Salmon live in the river. Buzzard, Kestrel and Owls nest in the con-ifer plantation; Pied Flycatcher and Red-start may be seen in the Sessile Oak woods in summer. Leaflet from: Maesgwm Visitor Centre (Gwynedd 9a) and on site.

☐10 miles/16 km south-east of Dolgellau on unclassified road off A487. OS 124: 769 093.

13 Great Ormes Head

Country Park with small local nature reserve. Spectacular peninsula of Car-boniferous Limestone with limestone pavement. Interesting plants including wild *Cotoneaster intergerrimus* (found only on this site) and typical limestone flowers such as Rockrose, Salad Burnet and Wild Thyme. The damp crevices in the limestone pavement provide a habitat for a wide variety of ferns. Butterflies on the cliff grassland include Grayling and Silver-studded Blue. Cliff-nesting birds such as Fulmar, Guillemot, Kittiwake and Razorbill may be seen here.

☐Coast road from Llandudno pier or walks from Happy Valley. OS 115: 783 832.

14 Gwydir Forest Trail

Forestry Commission. A walk through coni-fer plantations with some deciduous trees such as Sessile Oak, Beech, Sweet and Horse Chestnuts and Rowan. A variety of woodland birds (see page 12); Owls and Woodpeckers often nest in the Oak trees. Raven and Buzzard nest in the gorge of the Llugwy River below Swallow Falls. Mam-mals include Grey and Red Squirrels,

Stoat and Weasel. Leaflet from: Forestry Commission, Aberystwyth or Snowdonia National Park Centre, Betws-y-Coed.

□2½ miles/4 km west of Betws-y-Coed. Turn off A5 at Ty Hyll. OS 115: 759 578.

15 Gwydir Forest, Cae'n-y-coed Arboretum

Forestry Commission. A walk through woodland containing a wide and interesting variety of introduced conifers. Leaflet from: Snowdonia National Park Centre, Betws-y-Coed and on site.

□2 miles/3 km north-west of Betws-y-Coed on A5. OS 115: 763 576.

16 Gwydir Forest, Llyn Geirionydd

Forestry Commission trail in woodland near the lake. Mainly conifers with some deciduous trees such as Birch, Oak and Rowan. Forest birds (see page 12) and mammals including Red Squirrel, Stoat and Weasel. This is a former lead mining area and there are no fish in the lake due to the high lead content of the water. Leaflet from: Snowdonia National Park Centre, Betws-y-Coed.

□3 miles/5 km west of Llanrwst on unclassified road off B5106. OS 115: 762 604.

17 Gwydir Forest, Llyn Elsi

Various footpaths lead through Forestry Commission conifer plantations to open moorland and Llyn Elsi – a softwater mountain lake. Aquatic plants include Stonewort. A range of upland mosses may be found in the area.

□Walks start near Betws-y-Coed off A470. or A5. OS 115: 794 565.

18 Migneint

A wild area of heather moorland (see page 121). Many ground-nesting birds including Red Grouse, Lapwing, Meadow Pipit and Golden Plover. Other birds include Buzzard, Merlin, Black-headed Gull, Common Sandpiper and Grey Wagtail.

□5 miles/8 km east of Ffestiniog on B4391. Turn onto B4407 at Pont yr Afon Gam for access to the north of the area. OS 124.

19 Miner's Track, Snowdonia National Nature Reserve

A nature trail on an old track leading to and from disused copper mines. The area contains volcanic rocks and also traces of copper, gold, lead and zinc. Much of the vegetation is typical of acid grassland with plants such as Bog Asphodel and Sundew on wet ground and Heath Bedstraw and Tormentil on drier sites. A variety of flowers can be found on outcrops of base-rich rocks including Moss Campion, Purple Saxifrage and Wild Thyme. Mountain birds include Chough and Raven with Ring Ouzel in summer. Leaflet from: Nature Conservancy Council, Bangor.

□5 miles/8 km south-east of Llanberis on A4086. Start at Pen-y-Pass. OS 115: 648 558.

20 Mochras or Shell Island

Interesting peninsula with grassy sand dunes. Many seashells are washed up on the storm beach. Over 70 different species may be found; some of the more unusual include Chink Shell, Common and Turton's Wentletrap, Horse Mussel, Hungarian Cap, Keyhole Limpet, Pelican's Foot, Pheasant Shell, Prickly Cockle, Shipworm, Slit Limpet, Sunset Shell, Tower Shell, Tusk Shell, Violet Sea-snail and Wavy Venus. The best time to look for shells is during the spring and autumn tides. Many wild flowers grow here, especially dune plants such as Sea Holly, wild Dwarf Rose and orchids. Shelduck nest in the dunes; other birds that may be seen here include Common and Arctic Terns, Dunlin and Sandpiper. Seals may be seen swimming offshore. Morfa Dyffryn National Nature Reserve is south of the island.

□Cars can be taken onto the island at low tide. 7 miles/11 km north of Barmouth on unclassified road off A496 at Llanbedr. OS 124: 567 271.

21 Morfa Harlech National Nature Reserve

A sand dune system with dune slacks. A variety of plants on the dunes such as Bee and Pyramidal Orchid, Maiden Pink and Sharp Rush. Plants in the slacks include Marsh and Northern Fen Orchid, Moonwort

and Greater Bladderwort. Birds such as
Teal and Whooper Swan migrate here in
winter. The beach is an excellent site for
collecting shells (see Mochras, previous
entry, for examples).
☐Just north of Harlech on unclassified
road off A496. OS 124: 574 317.

22 Oriel Eryri
Interesting Environmental Gallery with
dioramas and modern displays on the
natural history of the Snowdonia area and
the effect of man on this environment. The
gallery has exhibits on geology, climate
and mountain and seashore life. Proposed
opening summer 1982/3 but open in summer 1981 for travelling exhibitions.
☐Llanberis, Caernarvon (Tel: Llanberis
636). Open daily. OS 115: 581 601.

23 Portmeirion
Interesting sub-tropical gardens and large
areas of woodland in the grounds of a holi-
day village. Fine collection of Azaleas,
Rhododendrons and unusual trees and
shrubs, which are best seen from May to
July. The mild winter climate, due to the
Gulf Stream (see page 9), allows shrubs
such as Mimosa to be grown here.
☐Portmeirion, Penrhyndeudraeth (Tel:
Penrhyndeudraeth 770453). Open daily,
April–October. 1 mile/ 2 km south-east of
Porthmadog on A497. OS 124: 589 371.

24 Trawsfynydd Nature Trail
A trail leading through the landscaped
grounds of a nuclear power station, alongside Trawsfynydd Lake. Islands on the
lake provide nesting sites for gulls and
Common Terns. Moorland birds include
Curlew and Wheatear (summer). Birds that
have been recorded in a stand of Beech
and Scots Pine include Buzzard, Sparrowhawk, Spotted Flycatcher and Willow
Warbler. The ravine of the River Prysor has
many ferns and mosses and birds such as
Dipper, Pied Flycatcher (summer), Redstart (summer) and Warblers may be seen
here. Barn Owls nest in this area. Leaflet
from: Central Electricity Generating
Board, Stockport.
☐3 miles/5 km south of Ffestiniog on A470.
OS 124: 698 384.

Anglesey

25 Cemlyn Bay
North Wales Naturalists' Trust nature
reserve (National Trust). A sheltered
brackish lagoon and damp fields separated from the sea by a shingle ridge. A
good birdwatching site, especially in winter. Birds that may be seen include Goldeneye, Little Grebe, Red-breasted Merganser, Oystercatcher, Redshank, Grey
Plover, Shelduck and Teal. Please do not
disturb nesting birds, particularly on the
shingle ridge.
☐8 miles/13 km west of Amlwch on
unclassified road off A5025. OS 114:
328 929.

26 Llyn Alaw
An excellent site for watching wildfowl in
winter; also waders during the spring and
autumn migrations. A bird hide is
available. There is also a Visitor Centre
with displays about the natural history of
the reservoir. Leaflets from: Head Ranger,
Llyn Alaw, Llantrisant, Holyhead.
☐7 miles/11 km south of Amlwch on
unclassified roads west off B5111 (north of
Llannerch-y-medd) and B5112. OS 114:
374 855.

27 Newborough Warren
National Nature Reserve
Nature Conservancy Council. An extensive sand dune system with an interesting
variety of plants including Wild Pansy,
Meadow Saxifrage and Wild Thyme on the
dunes and Grass of Parnassus, Dune Helleborine, Marsh Orchid and Wintergreen
in the slacks. Many mammals, lizards and
insects live on the dunes and Toads are
common. There are colonies of Herring
Gulls and other birds include Oystercatcher, Lapwing, Curlew and Meadow
Pipit. A rocky coastline with many seaweeds at Ynys Llanddwyn. Also Spring
Squill (see page 31) in grassy areas. Other
habitats on the reserve include the Cefni
Saltmarsh and Malltraeth Pool, which are
both good sites for wading birds and wildfowl (see page 30). Leaflet from: Nature
Conservancy Council, Bangor.
☐Visitors are asked to keep to six way-

marked paths through the reserve. Permits for other areas available from: the Warden, "Serai", Malltraeth, Bodorgan or Nature Conservancy Council, Bangor. 12 miles/ 19 km south-west of Menai Bridge on unclassified road off A4080. OS 114: 404 636.

28 Newborough Forest

Forestry Commission. The Hendai Trail explores this Site of Special Scientific Interest. Mainly Corsican Pine with a variety of wild flowers in forest clearings. Many birds and insects; mammals include Rabbit and Hare. Leaflet from: Snowdonia National Park Centre, Betws-y-Coed and on site.

□12 miles/19 km south-west of Menai Bridge on unclassified road off A4080. OS 114: 404 636.

29 Penmon Beach

A sandy shore with some rocks and seaweeds. Many burrowing worms such as Lug Worm and Sand Mason. Also burrowing Sea Anemones, Heart Urchins, Starfish and Razor Shells. Among the rocks, Soft Corals (Dead Men's Fingers), Sea Slugs and Feather Stars may be found. Gulls and waders, such as Dunlin and Oystercatcher, feed on the shore.

□8 miles/13 km north-east of Beaumaris on unclassified road off B5109. OS 114: 629 804.

30 Penrhos Nature Reserve

Penrhos Nature Reserve Association (Anglesey Aluminium Ltd.). An interesting reserve in the grounds of an aluminium plant. Wildfowl on the ponds include geese such as Barnacle, Canada, Greylag and Snow Goose. There is also an animal hospital on the reserve. The "Specialist Sector" covers a large area of scrub and saltmarshes on the shores of the inland sea. Unusual Tern colonies and many waders such as Black-tailed Godwit, Greenshank, Oystercatcher, Spotted Redshank and Whimbrel can be seen from hides in this area. Booklet from: the Warden's office, at address below.

□Permit needed for "Specialist Sector". Apply to: Police Constable Ken Williams MBE FZS, Penrhos Nature Reserve, Holyhead (Tel: Holyhead 2522). 1 mile/2 km south-east of Holyhead on A5. OS 114: 275 805.

31 Rhosneigr Beach

A rocky shore good for seaweeds and shells. A variety of waders such as Ringed Plover, Redshank, Turnstone and Oystercatcher can be seen on the sheltered shores around the rocks. Sea Holly and other coastal plants grow on the sand dunes to the south of the village.

□1 mile/2 km west of Llanfaelog on unclassified road off A4080. OS 114: 317 725.

32 South Stack

a) South Stack Cliffs RSPB Reserve

An interesting coastal reserve including the shore between North and South Stack, the headland of Penrhos Feilw Common and Holyhead Mountain. The best time to visit is in late May and June to see breeding colonies of seabirds and cliff plants (see also page 30). Rare heathland plants include Field Fleawort and Spotted Rockrose. Adder and Common Lizard can be seen on heath areas on sunny days. Unusual butterflies include Silver-studded Blue and Marsh Fritillary. Grey Seals may be seen in the sea. Leaflet from: RSPB, Newtown, Powys or South Stack Cafe. There is a warden on the reserve from April to September.

b) South Stack Nature Trail

The trail leads down the steps to the South Stack Lighthouse. Good views of seabird colonies and coastal plants from May to mid-July. Leaflet from: North Wales Naturalists' Trust or South Stack Cafe.

□3 miles/5 km west of Holyhead on unclassified road off A5. OS 114: 206 824.

33 Tre-arddur Bay

A very wide range of marine animals and seaweeds; a good place to study the zonation of rocky shores. A variety of animal life such as Crabs, Sea Anemones, Sea Mats, Sea Slater, Sea Squirts (see page 23), Sponges and Starfish.

□3 miles/5km west of Valley on B4545 on Holyhead Island. OS 114: 256 790.

Powys

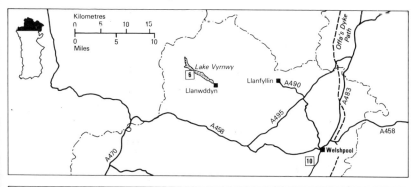

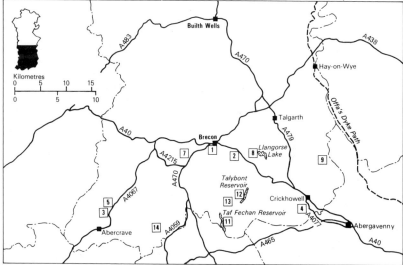

Offa's Dyke Path

The path winds to and fro across the border, crossing the Black Mountains, the Clun Hills and forest and passing along the Severn Valley. The path follows the dyke itself between Kington and Knighton. For details, see entry at beginning of Clwyd.

1 Brecknock Museum

Collection includes good displays on the natural history and geology of the surrounding area.

☐Glamorgan Street, Brecon (Tel: Brecon 4121). Open daily, except Sunday.

2 Brecon and Abergavenny Canal

Canal set in attractive countryside following the valley of the River Usk. A variety of waterside flowers, birds and animals and also aquatic insects (see page 18).

☐Access off B4558 between Llanfrynach and Llangattock. OS 161: 07 27 and 20 17.

3 Craig-y-Nos Country Park

The park contains a range of habitats: rivers, lakes, Beech woodland and meadows. Many wild flowers including Foxglove, Hemlock Water Dropwort, Marsh Marigold and Yellow Flag. A good site for birds such as Dipper, Goldcrest,

Great Spotted Woodpecker, Grey Heron and Kingfisher. Leaflet from: Brecon Beacons National Park Authority, Brecon. □Pen-y-cae, Upper Swansea Valley (Tel: Abercrave 395). Open daily. 18 miles/ 29 km south-west of Brecon on A4067. OS 160: 840 155.

4 Craig-y-Cilau National Nature Reserve
Nature Conservancy Council. A geologically diverse site rich in plant life. Four rare species of Whitebeam grow here. Many birds typical of open grassland (see page 15) and also Tawny Owl and, in summer, Redstart and Ring Ouzel. Leaflet from: Nature Conservancy Council, Aberystwyth.
□Please keep to the footpaths through the reserve. 8 miles/13 km west of Abergavenny on unclassified road off A4077 via Llangattock. OS 161: 185 168 and 201 161.

5 Dan-yr-Ogof Showcaves and Geological Museum
Extensive cave system in Carboniferous Limestone with stalagmites and stalactites. Also a small museum with minerals, fossils and a special display on caves.
□Abercrave, Glyntawe, Swansea (Tel: Abercrave 284). Open daily Easter – October, weekends only in winter. 4 miles/6 km north of Abercrave on A4067. OS 160: 838 161.

6 Lake Vyrnwy RSPB Reserve
An interesting reserve with a wide range of habitats including the lake, deciduous woodland, conifer forest, meadows and heather moorland. This is one of the few sites in Wales where Goosanders breed and many species of wildfowl visit the lake in winter. A variety of birds live in the wooded areas including Crossbill, Black Grouse, Siskin, Sparrowhawk and Woodcock. Buzzard and Red Grouse, Merlin and possibly even Hen Harrier may be seen on the moors. Mammals include Badger and Polecat. This is also a good area for butterflies in summer. Leaflets from: RSPB, Newtown, Powys and Information Centre on site.
□The Warden, Ty-Llwyd, Llanwddyn,

Oswestry. Public hide at north-east corner of the lake. Information Centre open weekends only Easter–May; afternoons daily June-September. 8 miles/13 km west of Llanfyllin. B4393 circles the lake. OS 125: 017 191 and 985 215.

7 Libanus Mountain Centre
Tourist Information Centre with exhibitions on the countryside.
□Libanus, Brecon (Tel: Brecon 3366). Open daily. 4 miles/6 km south-west of Brecon on unclassified road off A470. OS 160: 977 262.

8 Llangorse Lake
A rich habitat for wildlife. Plants include Bogbean, Fringed Water-lily and Yellow Flag. Many migrating birds may be seen including Greenshank, Pochard, Green Sandpiper and Black Tern (see also pages 16–17).
□7 miles/11 km east of Brecon off A40 on minor road to Llangasty Tal-y-llyn. OS 161: 133 262.

9 Mynydd Du Forest Trail
Forestry Commission. Trail leading through Ffawyddog Wood. Deciduous woodland and coniferous forest with birds such as Crossbill and Goldcrest. Meadow Saffron can be seen along forest rides in autumn. Leaflet from: Forestry Commission, Cardiff.
□9 miles/14.5 km north-west of Abergavenny on unclassified road off B4423 near Llanfihangel Crucorney. OS 161: 266 251.

10 Shropshire Union Canal
Parts of the canal between Berriew and Welshpool are good sites for plants such as Amphibious Bistort, Yellow Flag, Fleabane, Monkey Flower and Common Spotted Orchid. Birds include Kingfisher, Redpoll, Reed Bunting and Yellow Wagtail.
□Canal runs parallel to A483. Access by tow path. OS 136 and 137.

11 Taf Fechan Reservoir
Brecknock Naturalists' Trust. A good site for watching wildfowl in winter. Also many woodland birds in the forest on the west

side of the reservoir.
☐4 miles/7 km north of Merthyr Tydfil on unclassified road off A470. OS 160: 055 145.

12 Talybont Reservoir
Brecknock Naturalists' Trust. A local nature reserve and a good birdwatching site. Autumn visitors include Greenshank, Spotted Redshank and Ruff. Many wildfowl in winter such as Goldeneye, Goosander, Pochard and Whooper Swan. Typical birds of the surrounding hills are Buzzard, Raven and Ring Ouzel. Leaflet available from: Visitor Information Centre on site.
☐8 miles/13 km south-east of Brecon off B4558. Turn south onto unclassified road at Talybont. OS 161: 104 206.

13 Talybont Forest Trails
Forestry Commission. Walks exploring the woods near the headwaters of the River Caerfanell. Leaflet from: Forestry Commission, Cardiff.
☐On unclassified road leading south-west from Talybont Reservoir (see previous entry). OS 160: 063 170.

14 Ystradfellte
Riverside walks begin south of the village and follow the River Mellte through narrow limestone gorges with waterfalls. Sessile Oak woods with many ferns, mosses and liverworts. Leaflet from: Brecon Beacons National Park Authority, Brecon.
☐9 miles/14 km north-west of Aberdare on unclassified road off A4059. OS 160: 930 135.

Hill and Coastal Safety

Hill Safety
The weather on hills and mountains can change quickly, and it is always colder and generally windier at higher altitudes. Wind and rain on mountain tops can cause exhaustion and exposure. It is always advisable when going walking in hills and mountains to be well-prepared and be reasonably careful. Here are some guidelines:
● Don't be over-ambitious when planning walks, especially with children.
● Take note of weather forecasts and local information Notice Boards before setting off. Be prepared to change your route or turn back if the weather turns bad.
● Leave word with someone before setting off of where you intend to walk and how long you expect to be out.
● Wear or take with you warm clothing, including windproof and waterproof outer clothing, and headgear and gloves. Wear boots rather than shoes and never wear smooth soles, especially not smooth-soled rubber boots.
● A rucksack leaves your hands free for scrambling up and down steeper slopes. Carry the following items:
Good maps, preferably Ordnance Survey.
A survival bag or tent for shelter.

A compass: in misty conditions, using a compass may be the only means of finding your way back.
Energy-rich food such as chocolate and glucose sweets.
A basic first aid kit such as elastoplast, lint, antiseptic, crepe bandage.
An accurate watch, a torch and a whistle.
● Avoid crossing streams, except for very narrow, shallow ones. Avoid treading on scree or loose rock.
● In an emergency, six flashes of a torch or six blasts on a whistle is the signal that you need help.

Coastal Safety
Here are some suggestions to follow when you are walking along beaches or cliff paths.
● Find out the times of the tides – timetables are often sold in local shops.
● Keep an eye on the tide and don't get stranded.
● Watch out for crumbling paths on cliff walks.
● Avoid going too close to the edge of a cliff.
● Don't try and scramble down steep cliffs to reach remote beaches.

Conservation

Britain still offers a variety of habitats rich in wildlife, and areas of wild and beautiful countryside; but these areas are threatened as more land is taken up by industry, housing and agriculture.

When hedgerows are removed and woodlands are cleared, wetlands drained, heaths replaced by forestry plantations, and trees felled indiscriminately. The aim of wildlife conservation is to preserve existing habitats and manage them so as to ensure that the species dependent upon these habitats survive.

In Britain the official organization for the conservation of wildlife is the Nature Conservancy Council. They seek to inform farmers, planners and industrialists about environmental problems and to gain their co-operation in caring for the environment. The Council also protects important habitats by setting aside certain areas as nature reserves. County Naturalists' Trusts are important at the local level.

The ultimate responsibility for the survival of our wildlife lies with everyone, if the variety of countryside and wildlife is to remain and be enjoyed by future generations. The Countryside Commission has drawn up guidelines for visitors to the countryside. The main points are listed below.

The Country Code

Guard against all risk of fire.
Fasten all gates.
Keep dogs under proper control.
Keep to the paths across farmland.
Avoid damaging fences, hedges, walls.
Leave no litter.
Safeguard water supplies.
Protect wildlife, wild plants and trees.
Go carefully on country roads.
Respect the life of the countryside.

● *The Conservation of Wild Creatures and Wild Plants Act* makes it illegal to pick certain plants which are so rare as to be endangered, and to uproot *any wild plant* without the landowner's permission.

● *The Bird Protection Act* makes it illegal to take the eggs or disturb any wild bird at its nest.

Nature Conservation in Wales

The pressures on wildlife in Wales are more severe in the urban and industrial areas, which are mostly in the south of the country. Some habitats, such as the coastal wetlands near Cardiff, are directly threatened by development plans. Other areas suffer from the side effects of industrial processes. For example, the soil in the Lower Swansea Valley has long suffered from the accumulation of toxic waste and some of the rivers in South Wales have been polluted by coal dust.

Many coastal areas in South Wales have also been damaged by industrial pollution. The seawater in the Bristol Channel is contaminated by heavy metals and both the shore and the open sea near the oil terminal at Milford Haven have been badly affected by oil spills. Thousands of seabirds have been killed as a result of oil spills. The birds particularly affected are surface-swimming species such as Puffins and Guillemots.

Some steps are being taken to repair the damage caused by pollution. An Oil Pollution Research Unit at Orielton is studying the effects of oil on shore life and investigations into the types of plants that will grow in polluted soil have been carried out in the Lower Swansea Valley. As a conservation tool, it is essential that records are made so that future changes in the abundance and distribution of species will be noticed in time and remedial action taken.

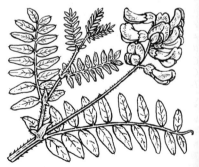

Upright Vetch was once common in old hay meadows but is now restricted to roadsides and field margins. This is probably due to changes in agriculture.

Useful Addresses

Central Electricity Generating Board,
Bird Hall Lane, Cheadle Heath, Stockport,
Cheshire.
Forestry Commission, Victoria House,
Victoria Terrace, Aberystwyth, Dyfed.
Forestry Commission, Churchill House,
Churchill Way, Cardiff, South Glamorgan.
Nature Conservancy Council,
Ffordd Penrhos, Bangor, Gwynedd.
Nature Conservancy Council,
Plas Gogerddan, Aberystwyth, Dyfed.
Nature Conservancy Council, 44, The
Parade, Roath, Cardiff, South Glamorgan.
North Wales Naturalists' Trust, 154 High
Street, Bangor, Gwynedd.
*RSPB (Royal Society for the Protection of
Birds)*, 18 High Street, Newtown, Powys.
Wales Tourist Information Centre, 3 Castle
Street, Cardiff.

Clwyd

Clwyd County Council/Nature Conservancy Council, Shire Hall, Mold

Dyfed

Dale Fort Field Centre, Dale, Near Haverfordwest.
Orielton Field Centre, Pembroke.
Pembrokeshire Coast National Park,
County Offices, Haverfordwest.
West Wales Naturalists' Trust,

7 Market Street, Haverfordwest.

Glamorgan

Cardiff City Council, King George V's
Drive East, Heath Park, Cardiff.
Glamorgan Naturalists' Trust, The Paddock,
Walterston, Barry.
West Glamorgan County Council,
12 Orchard Street, Swansea.

Gwent

Gwent Trust for Nature Conservation,
8 Pentonville, Newport.
Nurtons Field Centre, Tintern, Nr Chepstow.

Gwynedd

Snowdonia National Park Office, Penrhyndeudraeth.
The Drapers' Field Centre, Rhyd-y-Creuau, Betws-y-Coed.
Snowdonia National Park Study Centre,
Plas Tan-y-Bwlch, Maentwrog, Blaenau
Ffestiniog.

Powys

Brecknock Naturalists' Trust, Chapel
House, Llechfaen, Brecon.
Brecon Beacons National Park Authority,
Glamorgan Street, Brecon.
Dan-y-Wenallt Study Centre, Talybont-on-Usk, Brecon.

Further Reading

* *The Naturalist in Wales*. R. M. Lockley
(David and Charles: 1970)
Wild Wales. G. Borrow (Collins: 1977)
A Guide to the Birds of Wales. D. Saunders
(Constable: 1974)
Cambrian Forests. H. L. Edlin. Forestry
Commission Guide (HMSO London: 1975)
The Countryside of South Wales. H. Angel
(Jarrold: 1977)
* *The Snowdonia National Park*.
W. M. Condry (Collins: 1970)
The Natural History of Gower. M. E. Gillham (D. Brown and Sons: 1977)
The Dee Estuary – A Surviving Wilderness.
(Dee Estuary Conservation Group c/o
RSPB, Newtown, Powys)
Wales Walking. Wales Tourist Board
(1978)

Offa's Dyke Path. J. B. Jones. Countryside
Commission Guide (HMSO London: 1980)

**Countryside Commission National Park
Guides (HMSO London):**
Brecon Beacons No. 5. M. Davies (1978)
Pembrokeshire Coast No. 10. D. Miles
(1978)
Snowdonia No. 2. G. Rhys Edwards (1980)

**Publications of the National Museum of
Wales, Cathays Park, Cardiff:**
Welsh Wild Flowers. A. R. Perry (1979)
Welsh Seashells. J. E. Chatfield (1977)
Welsh Scenery. D. E. Evans (1972)

* Book now out of print but may be
obtainable from libraries.

Index

Welsh-English Glossary

aber	river - mouth	craig	rock	nant	brook
afon	river	croes/ groes	cross	nos	night
allt	hill, wood	cwm	valley	ogof	cave
arian	silver, money	dinas	hill, fort	oriel	gallery
bach	little, small	du	black, dark	pen	head, end
bannau	peaks, beacons	dyffryn	valley	pentre	village
betws	house of prayer	Eryri	Snowdonia	plas	hall, mansion
		ffordd	way, road	pont	bridge
brenin	king	glan	bank, shore	rhaeadr	waterfall
bryn	hill			sir	county, shire
bwlch	pass, gap	gwaun	moor		
cadair	seat, chair	gwyllt	wild	tal	brow, tall
		hir	long	tan/dan	under, below
caer	fort	hyll	ugly	traeth	beach
clydach	torrent	llyn	lake	tŷ	house
coch	red	maen	stone	tywyn	sand dune, seashore
coed	trees, woods	mawr	great, big	uchaf	upper, higher
		merthyr	martyr		
cors	bog	moel	bare hill	y,yr,'r	the
		morfa	saltmarsh	ynys	island
		mynydd	mountain	ystwyth	flexible

Acknowledgements: Photographers and Artists

Photographs and paintings are credited by page, left to right, running down the page.

Front Cover: Reinhard Siegal/Aquila, Heather Angel, E. O. Fellowes, John Mason, David Corke, (painting) Phil Weare/Linden Artists, June E. Chatfield. *Back cover*: John Sibbick/John Martin Artists.

Page 1: Heather Angel. *Page 3*: B. S. Turner. *Pages 4–7*: (maps) Swanston Associates. *Page 8*: John Woolverton. *Page 9*: June E. Chatfield (all three photos). *Page 10*: Andrew Cleave. *Page 11*: (painting) Victoria Goaman. *Page 12*: B. S. Turner, Andrew Cleave. *Page 13*: J. F. Young, E. O. Fellowes, E. O. Fellowes, J. F. Young, J. F. Young, J. F. Young, M. W. F. Tweedie/NHPA, Heather Angel. *Page 14*: David Corke, Brian Hawkes/NHPA, Geoffrey Kinns, R. T. Smith. *Page 15*: Heather Angel. *Page 16*: R. Shaw/NHPA, Heather Angel, E. O. Fellowes, Heather Angel. *Page 17*: B. S. Turner, J. F. Young, Heather Angel. *Page 18*: S. C. Bisserot, John Mason, John Mason, J. F. Young, J. F. Young. *Page 19*: Heather Angel, B. S. Turner. *Page 20*: A. F. Kersting. *Page 21*: J. F. Young, B. S. Turner, B. S. Turner, J. F. Young, M. Wright. *Page 22*: Dennis Avon & Tony Tilford, D. Green/Aquila, Donald A. Smith/Aquila. *Page 23*: R. H. Bridson, M. K. Lofthouse, J. F. Young, G. W. Ward/Aquila, Heather Angel, M. J. Woods, June E. Chatfield, June E. Chatfield. *Page 24*: June E. Chatfield, B. S. Turner, M. C. F. Proctor. *Page 25*: June E. Chatfield. *Page 26*: A. Barnes/NHPA, Dennis Avon & Tony Tilford, P. Scott/NHPA, B. S. Turner, Ray Kennedy/Aquila, J. F. Young, John Mason, John Mason. *Page 27*: (painting) John Sibbick/John Martin Artists. *Page 28*: R. Meams, Heather Angel, June E. Chatfield, Heather Angel, June E. Chatfield. *Page 29*: June E. Chatfield, June E. Chatfield, P. Scott/NHPA, Heather Angel. *Page 30*: R. H. Fisher/Aquila, J. F. Young, John Mason, Heather Angel. *Page 31*: John Mason, R. Balham/NHPA, June E. Chatfield, Stephen J. Krasemann/NHPA. *Page 32*: Frank V. Blackburn, John Mason, J. Blossom/NHPA, Geoffrey Kinns. *Page 33*: John Sibbick/John Martin Artists. *Pages 34–53*: Trevor Boyer. *Page 54*: Chris Shields/Wilcock Riley. *Page 55*: David Wright/Tudor Art, Chris Shields/Wilcock Riley. *Page 56*: Chris Shields/Wilcock Riley. *Pages 57–70*: Hilary Burn. *Page 71*: Hilary Burn, Michelle Emblem/Middletons, Hilary Burn. *Pages 72–78*: Hilary Burn. *Pages 79–80*: Joyce Bee. *Page 81*: Joyce Bee, Chris Shields/Wilcock Riley *Page 82*: Joyce Bee. *Pages 83–85*: John Barber. *Page 86*: John Barber, Michelle Emblem/Middletons. *Pages 87–8*: John Barber. *Pages 89–95*: Annabel Milne & Peter Stebbing. *Page 96*: Annabel Milne & Peter Stebbing, Bob Bampton/Garden Studio (Hawthorn). *Page 97*: Keith Preston. *Maps between pages 98 and 119*: Swanston Associates. *Page 122*: Andy Martin.